I0796755

‘Tim Patrick artfully explores the amazing depth and various entailments of the gospel. An accessible work for everyone on what the gospel is and what it means to read Scripture in light of the gospel. Patrick puts the pieces of the gospel-story and biblical-story in a way that many will find refreshing, illuminating, and deeply encouraging.’
Rev. Dr Michael F. Bird, Deputy Principal, Director of Research & Lecturer in New Testament, Ridley College, Melbourne

‘Every Christian knows the gospel. Right? Yet who among us does not hesitate when asked to articulate precisely what it is? What is its core, and where are its boundaries? This is the book you didn't know you needed, whether you're a newbie Christian or someone who preaches the gospel week in and week out. Tim Patrick has the theological mastery to make the most demanding doctrines digestible, and the pastoral heart to join the dots from each one of them to our actual lives. In the course of giving us a more conscious and confident grasp on the very foundations of our faith, *The Amazing Depth of the Simplest Truth* confronts us anew with the unexpectedness of what we believe, and leads us to marvel afresh at the good, good news of Christ crucified and risen.’
Dr Natasha Moore, Senior Research Fellow, Centre for Public Christianity

‘A valuable and accessible book that invites us to think deeply about the gospel in light of the Bible, theology and mission. Highly recommended for lay people, students and ministers to dive deeply into the good news of the cross and resurrection!’
Dr Andrew Abernethy, Assistant Dean of Bible and Theology Grad Programs, Professor of Old Testament, Program Director—M.A. in Biblical Exegesis, Wheaton College, Illinois

‘In *The Amazing Depth of the Simplest Truth* Tim Patrick invites us to taste and see the simplicity and riches of the gospel. Patrick's purpose is clear, he wants to grow our confidence and clarity in the gospel, to uncover its profound theological depth and reveal its practical implications for everyday life and ministry.

Patrick writes with the insights of a theologian, the heart of a pastor and the passion of an evangelist, resulting in a book that is engaging,

challenging and very accessible. While not afraid to urge us to reflect critically and dig deeper, Patrick's approach is balanced, nuanced and even-handed. This book will help to provoke reflection and spark conversation for anyone seeking to connect the good news of the gospel with the lives of those they disciple and evangelise.'
Lauren Hull, Senior Staffworker, Australian Fellowship of Evangelical Students

'This book rightly states that "nowadays, there are many different gospels circulating, even around relatively aligned Christian groups." Tim Patrick succeeds in bringing order to the chaos. Without polemics, Patrick maps out differing views and repeatedly arrives at a golden mean, not by compromise but by reaffirming biblical norms. With rigor, clarity and flair, this book will appeal to scholars, students and all others longing to press deeper into the gospel's amazing depth.'
Prof. Robert W. Yarbrough, Professor of New Testament, Covenant Theological Seminary, St. Louis, Missouri, USA

'It is often said that the proclamation of the gospel lies at the heart of Christianity, but it can be a surprise to discover how many people are unsure about what that gospel really is. The New Testament can be difficult to navigate, because its authors assumed that their readers already knew what the gospel was, and were usually more interested in correcting mistakes about it than in explaining it plainly and in detail. This book takes up the challenge of getting to the root of the matter, and tells us in simple but profound language what the gospel is, and why it is so important. In an age when we are bombarded by competing opinions, the need for such clarity is greater than ever, and here we have it. This is a book to instruct both the church as a whole and its individual members in the meaning of the eternal message of salvation in Christ. May it have a long and productive life in shaping the hearts and minds of those whose chief concern is to do what the apostle Paul did so long ago – to preach Christ and him crucified to a world that desperately needs to be brought back to God.'
Prof. Gerald Bray, Research Professor of Divinity, Beeson Divinity School, Alabama

'No quick fix here, but a deep dive into the way we should go about promoting the gospel of Christ. With clarifying summaries of leading Christian doctrines, and balanced yet sharp conclusions, Tim Patrick has given us an outline which is apologetic, evangelistic, systematic, pastoral and rhetorically elegant. Just what the gospel demands. It is a multi-faceted diamond and must reflect the grace of God through our beliefs and behaviours. I loved this book. Highly recommended!'
Rev. Canon Dr Rhys Bezzant FRHistS, Principal, Ridley College, Melbourne, Visiting Fellow, Yale Divinity School and Director, Jonathan Edwards Center Australia

'Dr Tim Patrick has written an essential and timely for Christians and scholars alike. *The Amazing Depth of the Simplest Truth* engages with clarity and theological depth, the core of the Christian faith. A vital book to navigate the confusion and distortion of the current age, equipping believers to understand, articulate and remain grounded in the true gospel of Jesus Christ.'
Chris Makin, Regional Director, Leading the Way Australia

'In this book, Tim Patrick has done the near impossible. He has crystallised the gospel in a way that captures both its depth and simplicity, whilst being neither parochial nor undiscerning. There is genuine profundity without unnecessary technicalities, and readability without being lightweight. There is self-awareness of assumptions and theological process without self-indulgence, alongside thoughtful biblical observations and schemas that work out in practical ways for Christian life and Christian ministry. I thoroughly enjoyed reading it, and I'm sure others will too.'
David Walter, Regional Director for the International Fellowship of Evangelical Students, South Pacific and Ministry Coach, Australian Fellowship of Evangelical Students

THE AMAZING DEPTH OF THE SIMPLEST TRUTH

Tim Patrick is Principal of the Bible College of South Australia, an affiliated college of the Australian University of Theology, where he lectures in systematic theology and practical ministry. Before moving into theological education and ministry formation, Tim served in local churches for ten years, pastoring several congregations and leading a number of revitalisation projects. Among his published works are *The Whole Counsel of God: Why and How to Preach the Entire Bible*, with Andrew Reid. Tim is married to Catriona and they have three children, Poppy, Jonty, and Remy.

THE AMAZING DEPTH OF THE SIMPLEST TRUTH

The Gospel and Gospel Theology

Tim Patrick

First published in Great Britain in 2025

Inter-Varsity Press
Studio 101, The Record Hall, 16–16A Baldwin's Gardens, London EC1N 7RJ
https://ivpbooks.com

EU GPSR Authorised Representative
LOGOS EUROPE, 9 rue Nicolas Poussin, 17000, La Rochelle, France
Email: Contact@logoseurope.eu

British Library Cataloguing-in-Publication Data
A catalogue record for this book is available from the British Library

ISBN 978-1-78974-585-6
eBook ISBN 978-1-78974-587-0

10 9 8 7 6 5 4 3 2 1

Typeset by Fakenham Prepress Solutions, Fakenham, Norfolk NR21 8NL

First printed in Great Britain by Clays Limited

eBook by CRB Associates

Produced on paper from sustainable sources

Inter-Varsity Press publishes Christian books that are true to the Bible and that communicate the gospel, develop discipleship and strengthen the church for its mission in the world.

IVP originated within the Inter-Varsity Fellowship, now the Universities and Colleges Christian Fellowship, a student movement connecting Christian Unions in universities and colleges throughout Great Britain, and a member movement of the International Fellowship of Evangelical Students. Website: www.uccf.org.uk. That historic association is maintained, and all senior IVP staff and committee members subscribe to the UCCF Basis of Faith.

For Cat,
my partner in the ministry of the gospel and in life.
With immeasurable love and thankfulness.

And
soli Deo gloria.

Contents

Preface

This book has been a long time in the making. Early in my ministry career, I served as an evangelist for a local church, and as part of that work I led a team in developing a course to train our congregations in outreach. Central to that project was helping church members to get a firm grasp on, and a clear picture of, the gospel. This was important because I had realised that, while our church taught the Bible and promoted straightforward Protestant theology, there were many believers in my circles who would express the gospel differently from one another, and some who could not confidently offer any articulation of it at all when they were directly asked. I suspect that this might be the case for many members of many churches today. While the course that we ended up developing saw some good use in our church, it was probably not as well-designed for its purpose it might have been. It did, however, prove to be of continuing value for me as I moved into a teaching role at a theological college. I found that the ground that the course had covered was relevant not only to my evangelism classes but also to many of my systematic theology lectures, and for me this highlighted something of the place of the gospel proper in wider Christian theology and some of the many connections between Christian theology and the straightforward proclamation of the gospel. With my background as a research scientist, the idea of a set of facts all being integrated around a well-defined controlling paradigm was both natural and exciting. I have been involved in these types of ministries over the past two decades or so, and one of my lasting aspirations has been to bring some of this framing and content together in a single and accessible volume as part of my service to the church.

I am therefore incredibly grateful for all of the people who have now enabled this project to be worked through, completed, and shared more broadly in a way that I hope will be of benefit to many individuals, churches and ministry organisations that are both committed to gospel clarity and convinced of the importance of integrated, biblical Christian theology. Thomas Creedy at IVP must be thanked for his excellence in continuously championing and managing the project, for his warm welcome of me, and for the stimulating conversations that we have shared over a number of great working lunches together. Bible College SA has been a truly wonderful base for my labours, with its highly supportive board and incomparable staff team, the former granting me a day a week to write and offering a generously supported sabbatical programme, and the latter doing so much to sharpen up and round out my thinking while always being just a fun and loving group to be part of. The Burrow Library at Bible College SA has been fantastic in supplying almost all of what I have needed throughout my writing, and the Bodleian Libraries were similarly helpful throughout my several months working in Oxford.

Then, for the rich and broad support that is needed to get through all of the fullness and complexity of week-to-week and year-after-year life, I am so grateful for my community of faith at Coromandel Valley Uniting Church. I could not wish for a more caring body of sisters and brothers in the faith.

And of course, I must acknowledge my wonderful family most of all, whom I love more than I am able to express. I am so thankful that God has put us together simply for the blessing that it is in itself, and for the ways that we can encourage and enable one another in our service of Jesus. At the heart of the family is my most precious wife Cat, and I could not imagine a better partner in life and in the work of the gospel. This book is not just better for her input; it would never have seen the light of day without her constant support, and I certainly would not be the person I am to sit down and write it apart from her. She is not only my pleasure but also one of the best influences in my life, as she helps me to grow in faithfulness and fruitfulness while showing such godly grace for all of the ways that I fall short. It is an honour to dedicate this book to her.

Finally, I give thanks to God, whose gospel and wider truths this book seeks to present for the ever greater glory of his only begotten Son Jesus, my Saviour, my hope and the source of my true identity. His graces are incalculable.

Introduction

The Apostle Paul opens his letter to the churches in Galatia by saying,

> I am astonished that you are so quickly deserting the one who called you to live in the grace of Christ and are turning to a different gospel – which is really no gospel at all. Evidently some people are throwing you into confusion and are trying to pervert the gospel of Christ. But even if we or an angel from heaven should preach a gospel other than the one we preached to you, let them be under God's curse! As we have already said, so now I say again: if anybody is preaching to you a gospel other than what you accepted, let them be under God's curse!
>
> Am I now trying to win the approval of human beings, or of God? Or am I trying to please people? If I were still trying to please people, I would not be a servant of Christ.
>
> I want you to know, brothers and sisters, that the gospel I preached is not of human origin. I did not receive it from any man, nor was I taught it; rather, I received it by revelation from Jesus Christ. (Galatians 1:6–12)

Paul's passion in this passage is crystal clear. He is passionate about the preservation of the genuine Christian gospel, the message that he and others have given themselves to spreading around the Mediterranean world of the first century. So precious is this gospel to Paul that he cannot fathom the idea that those who have accepted it might abandon it. And so critical to Paul is the purity of the message that he cannot abide the possibility of anyone, including even himself or an angel from heaven, contradicting it or distorting it. These, for him, are issues of the utmost importance. The apostle might seem intense in this matter, but his conviction makes sense in light of his belief that the gospel he proclaims is not a product of human imagination or speculation, but a direct revelation from Jesus Christ. Paul is therefore not being esoteric here; he sees the gospel as so vital and valuable precisely because that is how God sees it. If the gospel is a message from God to humanity – indeed, if the gospel is the primary message that God wants all people to hear, respond to and ultimately live by – then it would certainly be a grave and dangerous thing to distort or sideline it.

But as straightforward as Paul's words are here, what is stark by its omission is any outline of what the gospel message actually is. Despite using the word 'gospel' six times in this short extract of his writing, Paul does not define or unpack it. From this passage, we learn that the true gospel message is immeasurably important, but we have no clear idea as to what the message is! Presumably, Paul felt that he could leave this out of this letter because he knew that the Galatians already understood exactly what he meant when he spoke of the gospel. He was confident that its content, meaning and significance were well known by the Galatians because they had already been soundly instructed in these matters, at least in part by Paul himself when he took the gospel message through the region of Galatia on his first missionary journey (Acts 13–14). With this background, Paul knows that he does not need to outline or teach the gospel in this letter, and he can refer to it freely and safely in the knowledge that he and his audience understand each other on this point.

That is all well and good, but it might not be of much help to those of us who were not in Galatia in the first century when Paul passed through and gave instructions on the vital matters of faith. We are at potentially greater risk of lacking the same clear, precise, and agreed understanding of what the gospel is, and so we could ask whether we might also be more susceptible to unwittingly following a false gospel, or even of somehow altering the gospel when we speak of it to others. Almost all sincere Christians would be quite troubled by this thought – the last thing any of us wants to do is misunderstand or misrepresent God. Yet we need to consider soberly how we might do this unintentionally. One way might be through the relatively free use of the word 'gospel' without first establishing an agreed meaning for it. In some cases, we might do this naively, simply assuming that everyone means the same thing when they speak of the gospel, even if we have never actually explored whether or not that is so. In other cases, we might do it lazily, not wanting to put in the time or effort required to first of all clarify in our own minds what the gospel is and then to ensure that our understanding matches that of our interlocutors. Sometimes, we might even do it consciously but without too much concern, not believing that different understandings of the gospel make any significant difference to anything, especially if we presume that the differences are only minor, technical or perspectival. Whether or not we feel that we fall into any of these practices personally, the reality is that within the Christian world today, there is a very broad range of understandings as to what the gospel actually is, and a potentially even broader range exists among those who are not believers. Once again, contrary to the suggestion that this might not matter all that much, when we read over the opening lines of Paul's Letter to the Galatians, it would seem that it is in fact a major problem.

Somewhat frustratingly, it is also the case that this problem is not as straightforward to solve as we might like it to be. Although Christian believers with a high view of the Bible will agree that that is where we need to turn to confirm exactly what the gospel is, the answer is neither immediately clear nor unambiguous when we do so. As we have seen, biblical letters such as Galatians do not quickly tell us the gospel despite referencing it quite heavily. And if we chase the word across the rest of the New Testament, we find a great deal more of the same throughout. In fact, of the New Testament's more than 110 uses of 'gospel' words in their various noun and verb forms, the vast majority only reference the gospel without explicitly spelling out what it is. This is because, like Paul's Letter to the Galatians, significant parts of the New Testament are occasional and pastoral, written to those already in the faith and not primarily for the purpose of teaching the gospel to those who have never heard it. At least twenty-one of the twenty-seven New Testament texts clearly address audiences of believers. We might then wonder whether the other six books – the written Gospels of Matthew, Mark, Luke and John and the books of Acts and Revelation – are not like this and so should give us more direct teaching on the content of the gospel. But again, for the most part, where these texts use gospel words (incidentally, John never uses them in either his Gospel or his letters, and only uses them once in the book of Revelation), they also tend not to spell out their content but take it as already being understood by the first readers and hearers.[1] Of course, there are some important exceptions to this general pattern, and searching for the word is not the only way to determine the meaning of the gospel. These are points we will return to in some detail in the chapters ahead.

Resolving the true gospel turns out to be an issue at the academic as well as the popular level. Among scholars, a great deal has been written on the nature and content of the gospel in recent decades, much of it exploring new ground and some (although not all) of it springing from the debates around the so-called New Perspective on Paul. When Krister Stendahl, E. P. Sanders, James Dunn and others started questioning whether the Protestant tradition had interpreted Paul's message correctly, they started a movement that would continually probe and test the very heart of the Christian faith.[2] Paul proclaimed and taught the gospel. Thus, if the church had Paul's theology wrong, then it had the gospel wrong, plain and simple. Tragically, if correct, this would mean that the Protestant church at large wound up in the situation that Paul himself had warned so strongly against in Galatians 1. Some New Perspective scholarship therefore suggests that perhaps Martin Luther, from whom the Protestants inherited their framing of Paul back in the early sixteenth century, had been that 'angel from heaven' proclaiming a gospel contrary to that which Paul proclaimed.[3]

As stark and urgent as this challenge in the scholarship has been, it has stirred up much more than it has ultimately settled. Rather than offering up a single, neat and tidy corrective giving us a new and uncontroversial presentation of Paul's theology, something of an industry has grown up around New Perspective scholarship, and this is what has produced many of the new expressions of the gospel, each subtly different from the next. At the same time as all of this work has been going on, those who are unconvinced of the New Perspective's direction have done lots of their own work to reinforce the historical reformed conceptions of the gospel too.[4] The efforts have been extensive and the conversations lively, and while rank and file Christians might not be much aware of all of these goings on, there has certainly been a trickle-down effect. Pastors and teachers have thought through the issues during their time at seminary and then passed on their own particular positions to their flocks, who have in turn shared them with those investigating the faith. Likewise, ordinary believers wanting to keep growing in their understanding have gone directly to the wide range of more popular-level books on the gospel that have been on the market for many years now and have eagerly consumed their content. Again, not all of these have sprung out of the scholarship around the New Perspective; there are also many other theological conversations that have given rise to new understandings and articulations of the gospel over the previous century, and these too are to be found in the academy, the pulpits and the pews.[5] The bottom line is simply that, nowadays, there are many different gospels circulating, even around relatively aligned Christian groups.

In this context, there is a clear irony in the project of this book. On one level, it could be taken as yet another voice trying to be heard among the many already in the debate and trying to gain traction for yet another casting of the gospel. While there is a measure of unavoidable truth in this, the hope is that the present work is not quite that. First, while it will seek to go into some depth in some areas of Christian theology, it is not venturing all that far into the current debates, so the New Perspective on Paul will not be mentioned again, and the contours and priorities of that conversation have not been followed herein. Furthermore, no new gospel will be offered at all, only an affirmation of a view that is already mainstream and historically uncontroversial among evangelical believers. The only difference might be in the route taken to arrive at that view, a route chosen less for novelty and far more for the confidence that it is hoped it provides in the conclusion it reaches. Additionally, a repeated feature of this book will be an emphasis on the inherent theological balance of the gospel message, a balance that should bring together some of the helpful insights from several of the different views currently circulating. Together, all of this reflects the present goals of capturing the gospel cleanly without including anything in it that does not belong to it, while not excluding anything from it that does belong to it, and without foregrounding any one aspect of it at the expense of any others.

Beyond seeking to present the biblical gospel as clearly, reliably and even-handedly as possible, the other purpose of this book is to engage substantially with the meaning of the gospel, the theology that it both grounds and expresses and the connections between that theological meaning and the broader body of Christian theology of which it is the foundational part. The core premise is that, while the gospel consists of truths that are simple enough for almost anyone to understand, it is also amazingly theologically deep. Conversely, while Christian theology can be complex, profound and wide-ranging, it ought to be recognised as being fundamentally rooted in the basic message of the gospel. Structurally, this means that the first two chapters of this book will narrow down and do some very precise work, aiming to be as tight and accurate as possible on the essential summary of the gospel and to state the simplest truth of the Christian faith as plainly and accurately as possible. From there, chapters 3 to 5 move further into the gospel, and we will see that this simplest truth has that amazing theological depth. These chapters will present and affirm a number of the major doctrines of the faith, but they will do so by laying them out in the direct context of their flowing out from the gospel message, something that is not done often enough. At certain points, this will require a reframing of a number of common theological questions and the standard ways of answering them, and it will yield some potentially new insights too. At other points, it will mean bringing together things that are usually treated separately (for example, Christ's incarnation and resurrection) and teasing apart things that are sometimes blurred together (for example, the event and the meaning of Christ's death). This all represents an embracing of the freedom to organise and arrange orthodox theology in creative new ways, gospel-shaped ways, even without changing its substance.

Chapter 6 will touch on the completely unexpected nature of the gospel in all of its facets, even as it is the most fitting and natural culmination of the work of God, and here we will also briefly consider some of the implications of this for Christian ministry. In chapter 7, we will broaden out from the gospel proper and its immediate theological meaning to an exploration of the connections between the theology of the gospel and the greater body of standard Christian theology, including some suggestions about how these connections might be made more regularly when studying the Scriptures in different ways. Chapter 8 is a closer look at the relationship between the gospel and one particular Christian doctrine, the doctrine of sin, and shows how an understanding of the full gospel addresses the whole problem of sin, not just a single aspect of it. From here, there is a natural progression to chapter 9, which closes off the book by offering some suggestions as to how a good understanding of the gospel can be effectively folded into the works of ministry and indeed how it can usefully shape the ministry of the word. It was considered most important that the book close this way, embodying the conviction that all good theology should have a meaningful expression in Christian life and ministry and that all well-thought-through ministry will be directly grounded in well-thought-through theology. To divorce our theological understanding from our faithful service would be to separate what God has joined together throughout the Bible.

Ultimately, the great hope is that the pages and chapters ahead will serve as a useful resource for anyone who not only wants to be as clear as possible on the central gospel message, but who also wants to plumb that message, understand more of its depth, reach and nuance, and even consider it as the entryway to the fuller body of Christian theology. Given this aspiration, the study has been put together with accessibility as a priority. While this sacrifices some of the academic depth of other contemporary works on the gospel, it is hoped that more scholarly readers will still find some fresh and interesting material to engage with, while non-specialists will not be burdened with heavy technical matters, extensive footnotes or the need to bring a great body of prior knowledge to their reading. The gospel is God's good news for everyone, and so it should be within the reach of everyone as the simplest truth, even as it has the most amazing depth.

1
So. Many. Gospels.

We have already noted that, in spite of Paul's concern in Galatians 1, a proliferation of gospels is now taught throughout the worldwide church. In some cases, these gospels are quite like one another and obviously seek to articulate similar or largely overlapping sets of beliefs, even if they do so with different language or different emphases. In other cases, however, these gospels are quite at odds with one another and so directly force questions about which of them are mistaken and which one, if any, is the true, historical gospel. Given this context, we will begin by briefly noting some of the variety of gospels that have been put forward by different sectors of the wider church, before going on to consider some of the understandings of the gospel that exist today within the fold of self-identifying, traditional evangelical Christians.[1]

As we consider these alternatives, it will be important to remain quite strict with regard to the initial purpose of this work: our goal is not simply to separate true biblical teaching from false and to sift out heresy or heterodoxy from orthodoxy, but instead, to be as sharp and clear as possible about which parts of the Bible's teachings can and should be recognised as 'the gospel' itself. This is because our overall task includes investigating the structure and arrangement of Christian theology and its relationship to the gospel, rather than merely assessing the validity of any particular doctrinal claims. To put it another way, even if we decide that certain theological assertions do not belong under the heading of the gospel proper, this does not necessarily mean that they are untrue or unworthy of being championed and propagated by the church. It is of course vital for church leaders to sniff out and eradicate any teaching that is truly opposed to the gospel – and doubly so if that teaching is offered as the gospel. But in many cases, what is offered as gospel is not false teaching per se; it is only inaccurate to claim that it is the message of the gospel.

It is an unfortunate reality that there have been instances of God's people marginalising, relativising or even rejecting some of the plain lessons of Scripture as an overreaction to them being mistakenly promoted to the status of gospel. As one example, proactive works of social care have been largely abandoned by some quarters of the church for fear that participating in them might end up overshadowing the gospel of salvation or signalling to members of the church and the wider world that social action *is* the substance of the gospel. This is a great shame because even if some acts of community care do not constitute or communicate the gospel proper, they might still be good and right Christian practice, and perhaps even direct outworkings of the gospel, that ought to have expression in the ministry of the people of God. The desire for a church to be singly focused on the gospel is noble, but it is a mistake to suggest or imply that matters of secondary importance are essentially unimportant. Secondary importance is still extremely important in God's economy! Therefore, as we evaluate the different proposed gospels, error certainly needs to be corrected, lest the true gospel be displaced or lost altogether, but theological reconfiguration will often be the order of the day, not outright rejection.

Clearing the decks

For most evangelical Christians, the gospel – whatever its precise articulation – is at least assumed to be somehow about Christ's death and resurrection and their benefits for a trusting humanity. With this baseline in place, there are many framings of the gospel that will quickly be recognised as incorrect. It is not our current purpose to look at each of these proposals in any depth, but we can offer a pencil sketch of some of them here, with apologies in advance for the lack of nuance that a deeper study would allow and that some of their advocates might have wished for.

A quick glance over Western church history reveals that one gospel that has been consistently rejected by orthodox and reformed Christians is that which is now popularly encapsulated in the idea of 'salvation by good works'. An early example of this is found in the story of Augustine, the great North African bishop-theologian of the late fourth and early fifth centuries, who opposed the faith system of the British monk Pelagius – the latter maintaining that human beings had enough innate good within them to enable them to make a contribution to their own salvation. Augustine rebutted this by strongly asserting the doctrine of original sin and every human's complete dependence on the grace of God.[2] Nothing a person could do, claimed Augustine, would contribute to their salvation. It was all God's free gift.

Augustine won the day, but a millennium later, the common formulation of the Roman Catholic Church's view of salvation was that faith in God's grace was important, but it needed to be supplemented with various efforts and 'good works' in both the moral and ritual spheres of life as they were prescribed by that church. In response to this position, and the other perceived distortions in biblical faith that it caused, the theological programme of the sixteenth century's breakaway Protestants was shaped around what would later be labelled 'the five *solae*' (*sola* being Latin for 'alone'), which included faith alone, grace alone, and Christ alone and thus highlighted that any claim to salvation based on a person's own works was invalid, ignorant and even belittling of God. Although the reform movement flourished in the Western world, the gospel of salvation by good works never disappeared. Far from being a historical curiosity, versions of this teaching persist through to the present day in the Catholic Church, where the core doctrine has not changed a great deal since the medieval period. Of course, much of humanity outside of the committed Christian world also holds to forms of salvation by good works as an ultimate truth. This view underpins both mainstream agnostic and nominally Christian secular culture, as well as some of the major alternative formal belief systems such as Islam, Hinduism and Buddhism. Their common conviction is that a cosmic justice will at some point measure the quality of each person's life, and everyone will then receive either rewards or punishments commensurate with their actions.

Another family of gospel presentations can collectively be placed under the title 'salvation by tribe'. These presentations hold that God only accepts those who belong to a certain race, nation, brand of church or other subgrouping of people. Significant portions of the New Testament are given over to combatting an early expression of this view, specifically the idea that it is the Jews, with their particular history, customs, covenant and even bloodline, who are exclusively God's chosen people. While that understanding was quite reasonably drawn from the Old Testament, it is turned on its head by the Gospels' stories of Jesus welcoming many who were not Jews and rejecting others who were. The book of Acts and several of the New Testament Epistles similarly go to great lengths to show that there are no barriers of race, nationality, language, family, gender, class, qualification or anything else that can either bar people from or automatically qualify them for participation in Christ's community of faith.[3]

Despite this repeated and clear biblical teaching, versions of salvation by tribe are still alive and well today.[4] At one extreme, hyper-exclusivism is a characteristic of many pseudo-Christian cults and, distressingly, some forms of white supremacism have been undergirded by the bizarre belief that Caucasians are God's preferred people.[5] Similarly, claims have sometimes been made that certain of today's geopolitical units, including the US and UK, are God's 'elect nations'.[6] These ideas were fortified in the ages of the Enlightenment and the British Empire, but do not have any demonstrable scriptural backing and so are strongly rejected by most Christians. Sadly, however, it is only slightly more subtly that too many relatively mainstream Western churches still come close to anathematising others that differ on particular debated points of theology, or even just in their style. In fairness, some of these churches might take such decisions heavily and as a costly expression of their integrity, having concluded that, ultimately, those outside of their group are so mistaken that they have completely lost the core of the Christian message. Their lines are sometimes drawn over issues perceived to be of central importance, such as believers' baptism, sexual practices, certain experiences of the Holy Spirit, the ministry roles open to women or the interpretation of the Bible's creation accounts. For other churches, the circle is drawn even smaller, and there is no room for charitable disagreement even on questions of cultural engagement or church polity. Perhaps ironically, there are also some groups of Christians who define themselves by a commitment to *avoid* being dogmatically rigid on any point for fear that such rigidity can only lead to division, but who then find themselves slow to embrace other believers who do hold firm beliefs on certain theological issues. In all of these cases, tribal impulses serve as much to exclude as to include people in the gospel family.

The opposite of salvation by tribe is what could be called the gospel of 'radical inclusivity' or universalism.[7] As well as having some scholarly advocates, this is a common liberal and pop gospel that maintains that, in the end, all people will be received by God irrespective of their particular beliefs or behaviours. Sometimes, this is presented as the natural outworking of the proposition that God is love: if God's love is central to his identity, then this can only be expressed in his loving act of accepting and saving all people without distinction (1 John 4:8, 16). But many evangelicals are quick to point out that this interpretation is impossible to square with a great deal of the Bible's teaching, especially the imperatives for evangelism ('What need is there to call people to turn to God if everyone will be accepted anyway?') and the stark warnings about rejecting the call of God, which are even found on the lips of Jesus.[8] Theologically, we could say that radical inclusivity is unsatisfactory, as it seeks to play off one of God's attributes against the others, here using his love to override his holiness and justice, rather than understanding all of God's attributes as harmonious expressions of his non-contradictory and undivided reality.[9]

For their significant differences, what is common to the three types of gospels sketched above is the primacy that each places on eternal salvation. Whether by works, by tribe or by the comprehensive scope of universalism, their concern is for a post-mortem deliverance from any judgements or punishments and for delivery into lasting peace and paradise. But not every proposed gospel has salvation as its ultimate goal. Some place more temporal concerns front and centre.

One example of this is the so-called prosperity gospel with its underpinning conviction that God's great purpose is to bless his faithful people in physical and material ways in this life. The promises of some expressions of this gospel include that believers in Jesus can expect to be kept safe from adversaries, healed of any infirmities and even made rich. These ideas are primarily developed from the Old Testament, where the Israelite people are indeed promised these kinds of rewards for their faithfulness, but they do not account so well for the balance of the New Testament's teaching, which on the one hand showcases many miraculous healings performed by Jesus and the apostles, but which on the other hand repeatedly makes plain that the church of God should expect significant persecution and suffering for following Jesus in this life, even as it encourages hope in the life to come where all needs and longings will be satisfied.[10] The New Testament never abandons the Old Testament hope, but it also redirects the aspirations of God's people to the eternal fulfilment that earthly blessings can only foreshadow.[11]

Another more temporally focused collection of gospels are known as the 'social justice gospels', which present the Christian message as essentially the requirement to do what is right and good for others and to establish communities that bless wider communities.[12] These gospels call on believers to be active in the political arena, through community-based programmes or enterprises, or by caring for the needy at a more interpersonal level. There are many different expressions of these beliefs, and some of them narrow down to seek justice for one particular group of oppressed or marginalised people (for example, women, people of non-traditional sexualities, certain ethnic groups, disabled people, refugees or the poor) with entire theological structures sometimes being developed around these causes – such as feminist theology, queer theology, Black theology and liberation theology.[13]

As discussed above, it is quite possible – and indeed inescapably explicit – that the Bible repeatedly enjoins Christians to engage proactively in sacrificial social service and love for others, including the oppressed and the othered. Yet many Bible readers will note that while the imperative to 'do good unto others' is central to Christianity and so is sometimes framed as 'the golden rule', it does not seem to constitute the primary emphasis of the Christian gospel (cf. Matthew 7:12; Luke 6:31). If it did, the Christian life would only be about following a system of ethics, something broadly interchangeable with the basis of most civil societies. This might well be the most excellent way for people and societies to live, but as a system for attaining salvation, it is ultimately just another version of justification by works.[14]

Today's evangelical gospels

Most evangelicals will not require much, if any, convincing that the beliefs surveyed above do not reflect the biblical gospel, even if some of them do resonate with important biblical truths. But despite a general agreement about which so-called gospels are inadequate or off target, it is sobering to recognise that even within the evangelical camp, there is no broad consensus today on a sharp definition of what the true gospel is.[15] Most do agree that Jesus' death is central, but even that is not unanimously held, and its meaning is certainly debated – something that we will explore in chapter 4. Some gospels also variously include human sin, Jesus' earthly ministry, his resurrection, and the need for faith and repentance, although the latter two might sometimes be recognised as responses to the gospel rather than the gospel itself. As we now examine some common evangelical articulations of the gospel in more depth, we must again note that while these might not be in any sort of formal contradiction in terms of their separate points of doctrine – most of their proponents believe very similar things – the emphases and structural differences are not insubstantial. Of course, we cannot attempt to consider every published articulation of the gospel here. That would take several books. Instead, our approach will be to interact with the works of a few respected and influential writers, who have captured some of the major positions that are current within evangelical thinking.

It is helpful to begin by recalling that during the 1950s and 1960s, it had become critical for Western evangelicals to defend their convictions regarding the centrality of the cross of Christ in response to both theologically liberal scholarship and the ecumenical movement, which were both charting novel paths for Christian doctrine. In this context, leading churchmen and writers such as John Stott and Leon Morris produced seminal works arguing for both popular and more academic audiences that Christ's death on the cross is the very heart of the gospel and central to the message of the entire New Testament.[16] Such writings were welcomed by evangelicals and have formed part of the theological bedrock of our movement ever since. But as vital and beneficial as some of these works were, it seems that, in some cases, their authors overstated their claims, as there is always a risk of doing when working in reaction to troubling alternatives. A good example of this overreach can be found in Stott's short commentary on the book of Acts. Addressing the question of whether or not Paul's Areopagus speech in Acts 17:22–31 can be considered a gospel presentation, Stott writes,

> I believe Paul did preach the cross in Athens. Luke provides only a short extract of his speech, which takes less than two minutes to read. Paul must have filled out this outline considerably, and his conclusion (30–31) must have included Christ crucified. For how could he proclaim the resurrection without mentioning the death which preceded it?[17]

For Stott, a valid gospel presentation necessarily includes the cross, and so this text – which appears to record a gospel presentation but nowhere mentions the cross – needs to be glossed to account for its obvious omission. Stott here concludes that Paul's original words 'must have included Christ crucified' even though, for some reason, Luke chose not to record that. Aside from raising some uncomfortable hermeneutical questions, Stott's interpretation leads us to ask if he has explored the possibility that perhaps Paul was not preaching the gospel at the Areopagus, or that the resurrection – the clear subject of the passage – is the central event of Paul's gospel, or that Paul did not believe that it was essential to mention the cross every time he gave a gospel presentation. Were one of these alternatives correct, it would not demonstrate that the cross was unimportant to Paul – that claim would be impossible to sustain in light of the rest of Paul's writing. It could just show that, for Paul, the cross and the gospel did not sit together in exactly the way that Stott believed that they did at the time when he penned his commentary.[18]

The idea of a singularly crucicentric understanding of the gospel carried forward in evangelical thought. In his volume *Apostle of the Crucified Lord*, New Testament scholar Michael Gorman writes,

> This fixation on a 'dead criminal' or even a dead Messiah sounds narrow, if not morbid. Where is the 'good news' without the resurrection? To be sure, Paul's gospel was not good news to him, and would not be good news to anyone else, without the resurrection

> … Nevertheless, it is absolutely crucial for Paul that his gospel be understood as centred on Christ crucified … This means that although the cross must be narrated and understood in connection with other events in the story of Christ and the larger story of Israel's God, those stories are themselves, for Paul, to be understood through the interpretive lens of the cross. The resurrection makes that perspective both *possible* and *necessary*.[19]

Here, not only is Christ's death the centre of the gospel and the overarching message of the Bible, but the resurrection is also offered as an event that only confirms that the cross must be taken in this way.

Other writers do not disagree with the importance of keeping the cross in sharp relief as the gospel is articulated, but they also contest that speaking of the cross *alone* is not enough to capture the wholeness of the biblical gospel.[20] These writers argue that while the gospel includes, and might even centre on, Christ's death, the cross and the theology of the cross do not constitute the *entirety* of the gospel. C. H. Dodd, a significant contributor to our understanding of the biblical gospel, takes this view in his seminal work *The Apostolic Preaching and its Developments*, where he puts forward his understanding of the content of the New Testament *kerygma*, or gospel proclamation. Beginning with 1 Corinthians 15:1–5 and drawing from Paul's other writings, Dodd summarises,

> The Pauline *kerygma*, therefore, is a proclamation of the facts of the death and resurrection of Christ in an eschatological setting which gives significance to the facts.[21]

Thus, for Dodd, both the death *and* resurrection of Christ are at the heart of the gospel. However, Dodd does not finally settle on just these two events, but also says, 'The *kerygma* as we have recovered it from the Pauline epistles is fragmentary.'[22] He suggests that it can be restored more fully as the following seven events or propositions:

- The prophecies are fulfilled, and the new Age is inaugurated by the coming of Christ.

- He was born of the seed of David.
- He died according to the Scriptures, to deliver us out of the present evil age.
- He was buried.
- He rose on the third day according to the Scriptures.
- He is exalted at the right hand of God, as Son of God and Lord of quick and dead.
- He will come again as Judge and Saviour of men [*sic*].[23]

But even this, for Dodd, is not the entire gospel proclamation. He goes further, saying, 'The apostolic Preaching as adopted by Paul may have contained, almost certainly did contain, more than this.'[24] This open-ended understanding of the events that constitute the gospel is encouragingly humble, but at the same time it is unhelpful to the project. According to this view, what would prevent us from suggesting that the gospel also includes Jesus being led by the Spirit, the sum of his teaching, his miraculous works, his human emotions, or other truths we find of him in the written Gospels? Where is the limit on what counts as gospel?

Some do indeed suggest that the Christian gospel message encompasses everything in the canonical texts of Matthew, Mark, Luke and John. The Christian scholar, author and podcaster John Dickson makes this argument from places such as Mark 1:1 and Matthew 26:6–13.[25] But Dickson then draws from the Gospel narratives, as well as the speeches in Acts and the so-called proto-creeds in the epistles, to suggest that five sets of events can be distilled as a summary of the gospel. They are:

- Jesus' royal birth secured his claim to the eternal throne promised to King David.
- Jesus' miracles pointed to the presence of God's kingdom in the person of his Messiah.
- Jesus' teaching sounded the invitation of the kingdom and laid down its demands.
- Jesus' sacrificial death atoned for the sins of those entering God's kingdom.
- Jesus' resurrection vindicated him as the Son whom God has appointed over his kingdom.[26]

This list of events largely overlaps with Dodd's, but there are differences. The birth, death and resurrection of Christ are common to both, but Dickson includes Jesus' miracles and teaching and excludes his return to judge, thereby placing more importance on his earthly ministry than the future consummation of his kingdom.

This variation leads us to note two very important things. First, because the written Gospels are so long, any claim that the gospel message captures everything that they say will require an attempt to condense and summarise them down as Dickson has done. Second, we must recognise that any such summarising will necessarily require us to make some critical judgements. Dickson has decided that the appropriate ways to crystallise the gospel message from the written Gospels is to filter the latter through the speeches in Acts and the New Testament's proto-creeds, but we can fairly ask why this is the best approach. We have already seen that the interpretation of the speeches in Acts is subject to pre-existing theological biases, and there is also debate around the New Testament's proto-creeds. Not only is the identification of such a proto-creed sometimes speculative, it is also unclear that the early church put nothing other than the gospel proper into its hymns and liturgies. It is quite conceivable that other important truths were also set and shared in this way, just as they still are today in our church songs and doctrinal confessions.[27] Equating the gospel with the Gospels sounds logical and promising at first, but the work of filtering out the core message can be quite complex and subjective.

Offering the gospel as the summary of an even broader block of the Scriptures, or indeed of the whole Bible, is another common approach that some scholars have taken. Scott McKnight, for example, openly looks to more than just the written Gospels and factors into his gospel the longer scriptural arcs that focus on all humanity and Israel, for which Jesus is the climax and fulfilment. Although McKnight does not really like the idea of boiling the gospel down into bullet points, he offers a multipage précis of it that traces the entire biblical metanarrative from creation to new creation.[28] This can be further condensed as follows: God created the world and designated human beings to be his under-governors, but humanity repeatedly fell afoul of God by attempting to usurp his ultimate rule. Finally, God sent Jesus as the true king, who paid the price for humanity's sins in his death and then rose again to continue ruling eternally. Those who accept Jesus as king receive the Holy Spirit who enables them to take up the original charge to rule on God's behalf, rather than in his place, more properly. At the last, Jesus will return, the world will be transformed and 'humans will govern on God's behalf in the way of Jesus'.[29]

McKnight's gospel contains many doctrinal assertions, and it identifies a problem and outlines the solution to that problem – the problem being humanity's attempt to wrestle authority from God. But it also casts all of this as a story, very helpfully reflecting the fact that the Bible unfolds a great narrative and that this is the primary form in which God has chosen to reveal his truth. McKnight is effectively calling us to recognise that the gospel is the story of the whole Bible, and the story of the whole Bible is the gospel, such that reading through the whole Bible gives us the gospel. However, it turns out that others can agree with this much and yet still end up finding a gospel with a noticeably different flavour. For example, Washington-based pastor Mark Dever, in his popular-level title *The Gospel and Personal Evangelism*, spells out the gospel as a summary of the whole Bible story centred on the life and death of Jesus:

> Here's what I understand the good news to be: the good news is that the one and only God, who is holy, made us in his image to know him. But we sinned and cut ourselves off from him. In his great love, God became a man in Jesus, lived a perfect life, and died on the cross, thus fulfilling the law himself and taking on himself the punishment for the sins of all those who would ever turn and trust him. He rose again from the dead, showing that God accepted Christ's sacrifice and that God's wrath against us had been exhausted. He now calls us to repent of our sins and to trust in Christ alone for our forgiveness. If we repent of our sins and trust in Christ, we are born again into a new life, an eternal life with God.[30]

While McKnight and Dever's presentations both aim to relate the central story of the same Bible, there are significant differences in how they condense that story, those differences being determined by their different interpretive grids. Once again, subjectivism results from attempts to summarise. McKnight, on the one hand, has narrated a story about competing exercises of, and claims on, power. The drama revolves around the question of who will rule. Dever, on the other hand, speaks of a recalcitrant humanity and their need for, and the means of, salvation. His question is about how sinners can be forgiven and restored. While these readings might not be in formal contradiction and could be taken as two complementary themes that run through the biblical narrative, they are offered not as different valid perspectives among many, but as definitive readings. Different writers follow different theological undercurrents that pull in different directions and lead to different places. This last observation also leads us to something else that is important to recognise when seeking to understand the gospel.

It is critical to see that the biblical gospel can be, and needs to be, addressed at two distinct levels: as events or sets of events, and as the theological meaning of those events. There is a history of happenings, and then there is the interpretation of the meaning of that history.[31] We need both of these layers to understand the gospel, and it is very helpful to distinguish between them as we seek to identify the gospel and assess the various presentations of the gospel.

Events and interpretations

So far, we have mainly been asking which events or story arcs different writers include in their summaries of the gospel, but we can now also go back to note the particular theological positions from which some of them make sense of those events.

For Dever, the interpretive grid is clearly the atonement and soteriology. His paragraph-long gospel (quoted above) includes far more than the cross, but all of the events he lists are tied into the story of the atonement, which centres on the death of Christ. The resurrection is included, but its purpose is merely to confirm that the cross achieved its purpose, and beyond this there is no indication that it adds anything of substance to the gospel's message in itself.[32] As we have seen for McKnight, the gospel events are not primarily understood as expressing or contributing to soteriology, rather they engage the issue of authority. He sees the big question of the Bible as being, 'Who reign and rules?'

and the answer that the gospel supplies as 'King Jesus'. As it happens, McKnight does ultimately boil his understanding of the gospel down to the pithy statement 'Jesus as Messiah and Lord is the gospel.'[33] Finally, Dodd is explicit in saying that the events of the gospel, however many there might be, must be taken in 'an eschatological setting which gives significance to the facts'.[34] This is all to say that the message of Jesus is not primarily about the forgiveness of past sins, nor about the recognition of Jesus as King or Lord, but about the future that Jesus opens up for his followers, including the prospect of a final judgement, which we noted that Dodd includes as one of his seven gospel events while Dickson leaves it out of his five.

Just by looking at these few writers, we see that the evangelical gospels do not only differ in the particular events or sets of events that they do or do not include, but they also prioritise different macro-doctrines.

While many other evangelical articulations of the gospel also express a theological priority for either atonement, the lordship of Christ or eschatology, there are some that stand out for recognising more than a single primary doctrinal line running through the gospel message. For example, in *The Crucified King*, Jeremy Treat makes the strong point that the doctrines of soteriology *and* the kingdom of God are both needed to understand the good news.[35] Indeed, Treat argues that because Jesus is the crucified Messiah, atonement cannot be understood apart from his rule, nor his rule apart from atonement, and shows that the tradition of isolating these two areas of theology has been singularly unhelpful. Similarly, in what might be one of his most important books, *The Resurrection of the Son of God*, N. T. Wright claims that the gospel sits at the theological intersection of Christology and the eschatological event of Jesus' resurrection. Commenting on Romans 1:1–4, and countering the idea that the gospel is the theological message of justification by faith, Wright says,

> The 'good news' Paul has in mind is the proclamation of Jesus, the Davidic Messiah of Israel, as the risen lord of the world.[36]

Here, for Wright, the gospel is not just that Jesus is Lord (as with McKnight's emphasis on the question of who rules) nor just that Jesus is risen (as with Dodd's eschatological focus), but that Jesus is the *risen Lord*, bringing both Jesus' sovereignty and eschatology together as the theological meaning of the gospel message.[37]

Such approaches might be more nuanced and balanced than those that mostly follow a single theological track, but we are still in need of a reliable means of adjudicating between views such as Treat's, which encompass soteriology and authority, but do not foreground eschatology, and Wright's, which highlight eschatology and authority but leave out soteriology. And more than this, we need to justify the assumption that soteriology, eschatology and authority are the right theological categories for the gospel in the first place.

Without yet attempting to resolve these matters, we ought to once more underscore two important points. The first is that the differences between the various evangelical articulations of the gospel mostly reflect the different emphases given to particular theologies and the alternate ways in which those theologies are brought into relationship with one another. Given this, we cannot for a moment suggest that anyone who champions, say, an eschatologically focused gospel does not therefore believe in the atonement, nor that someone who finds the atonement to be central therefore denies the lordship of Christ, nor that the foregrounding of the lordship of Christ is a rejection of biblical eschatology. The real issues for us are about how these theologies fit together and whether they couple with particular events that ought to be recognised as central events of the gospel proper.

The second point to note is that the theological layer of the gospel can tend to be more important for some than the identification of a tightly bounded set of historical gospel events. This is plainly the case for Dodd, who is confident in the eschatological meaning of the gospel, even if he cannot finally pin down every event proclaimed as part of the gospel by the early church. It would also appear to be the case for Dever, who includes Christ's resurrection in some of his expressions of the core Christian teaching, but not in others, with that change having no effect on the soteriological core of the message. Similarly, McKnight can present his gospel's pervading theology of authority either in a potted overview of the gospel story, rich with events from the history of God's people, or ultimately in a pithy statement of Jesus' lordship that does not mention any historical happenings all. This observation provokes a very important hermeneutical question: if the theology of the gospel is somewhat independent of a particular, clearly defined set of historical events, from what does the theology arise? Or, to ask the same question from the opposite direction: if some historical events can equally be either included in or excluded from an articulation of the gospel, in what ways do those events have bearing on the theological understanding of the gospel, and how are they meaningfully part of the gospel?

As we move forward in this book, it will be our purpose not only to explore the two layers of the gospel – the events and their theological meanings – but also to show that they are necessarily interdependent, with meaning flowing from the events and each event infused with meaning. If the gospel is the proclamation of a set of historical events, each with paramount theological significance, then a tight and economical articulation of the gospel should allow the relationship between these things to become clear.

2
The gospel from exegesis

Having surveyed a number of potential articulations of the gospel coming both from within the evangelical world and from beyond it, we will now start to move towards our own assessment as to which articulation best captures the heart of the Bible's message. To begin this process, it is vital that we first consider our approach or method. This is because in every field of study, methods greatly affect outcomes, and so determining the most appropriate way of answering the question of what the gospel is, is the critical first step to being able to settle on a conclusion that we can have confidence in.

Method matters

Given that all evangelical Christians look to the same Bible to determine the gospel message, we might have anticipated that they would all straightforwardly arrive at the same conclusion, but we have found that this is not at all so. In some cases, the differences are stark. In other cases, they are more subtle but still nonetheless real. We have also found that one major reason for these differences is that not everyone approaches the Scriptures with the same theological grid, and doctrinal convictions influence our investigations in at least two ways.

First, they affect interpretation such that coming to a text with a strong theological paradigm can sometimes result in meaning being read into a verse or passage rather than out of it. We perhaps saw something of this in the previous chapter, where authors were confident of the theological meaning of various parts of the Scriptures even if others would not immediately read the texts the same way. The cross was found where it was not mentioned, a variable selection of events in Jesus' life were all read through a common eschatological framework, and the entire variegated storyline of the Bible was recognised as majoring on matters of authority and rule. None of this is surprising, of course. It is an inescapable fact that there are no purely objective interpreters; the only people who read the Bible are people who already believe things. But it is good to recognise the bias that theological pre-conviction can bring, as this awareness at least increases the possibility of self-correction or fresh discovery.

The second way that a standing theological position influences investigations of the gospel is through text selection. Someone with a strong view that the Bible's central message is atonement is more likely to prioritise texts that speak clearly of Christ's cross, substitution, forgiveness and the like when they present the gospel. Someone who believes that the gospel is fundamentally eschatological might emphasise the importance of texts that detail the resurrection, the coming of judgement, the future hope and so on. Someone who maintains that the Scriptures' main concern is authority could give more attention to the passages that most loudly speak of things such as submission, allegiance, rebellion and other related topics. Of course, in all of these cases, there is as much chance of confirmation bias as there is of arriving objectively at the biblical gospel.

Given the last point, it might seem at first as though the move away from investigations grounded in the assessment of those short passages that are deemed to be critical to the question and towards studies based on larger and larger swathes of the Bible would help to solve the problem. Surely the more comprehensively the Bible is brought into the discussion, the less chance there is that select small sections will be able to influence our understanding disproportionately. But while there most certainly is some truth in this, and while we want to advocate for engagement with the whole Bible and the reading of each part of it in its wider context, significant theological bias can remain even with this approach, as we have already seen. It is equally possible to read the entire Bible through one of the lenses of atonement, eschatology or authority, and no doubt of other macro-doctrines too. We find quite different summaries of the message of entire Bible when different decisions are made about which passages are programmatic, which narrative lines are the most important and which themes are dominant. This is simply the unavoidable reality of attempting to condense the message of any large text, and it is worth keeping in mind. While it is fair in the natural sciences to assume that more data generally gives better results, the overriding power of subjectivity in interpretation means that when studying texts, starting with more data might not be more helpful in every case.

If focusing on individual texts is too narrow and open to selection bias, and if reviewing the whole Bible does not relieve this issue in any significant way, how are we to identify the gospel? Is there any suitable method of investigation? It might in fact be that we ought not to dismiss the prioritisation and examination of smaller, individual passages too quickly, especially if we could have a reasonable degree of confidence that any of them unambiguously tells us the gospel. While an orthodox doctrine of Scripture does not let us use one text to contradict, overrule or dismiss others, neither does it preclude individual texts from making large claims. So, if we were able to find a statement in the Bible that plainly and directly states, 'The gospel is *x*,' then surely we ought to accept *x* as the gospel. We ought to accept it even if it takes us time to work out how exactly *x* squares with the whole biblical narrative, with various theological themes, or with other verses and passages that we had always assumed carried the gospel, but do not immediately seem to line up neatly with *x*.

Of course, many of the short passages that get prioritised in investigations of the gospel are purported to do exactly this – to give us pithy summaries of the gospel. The problem is that, upon close inspection, it is not always unquestionably clear that all of these passages do in fact present the gospel proper rather than other biblical truths. In short, they might say good and important things, but it is often a matter of judgement as to whether those things actually constitute the formal gospel. Even after we work through issues of translation, context, structure and background, we still might not come to complete certainty that the text being examined was intended by its author to be a summary of the gospel.

This means that even a famous verse such as John 3:16 cannot simply be assumed to present a gospel summary. Despite its popularity and the indisputably important things it teaches, the verse itself does not make the claim that it is relaying the gospel. It *might* be that it is, but we have no exegetical evidence for this either from the text or the wider passage in which it sits. Similarly, 1 Timothy 1:15a, one of the five 'trustworthy sayings' found in Paul's letters to Timothy and Titus, might very well capture some gospel truth, but we have no way of confirming that this particular trustworthy saying is definitely the core of the gospel. Indeed, the fact that some of the other trustworthy sayings are clearly *not* the gospel means that that formula is not a reliable gospel marker.[1] Following the same logic, we cannot automatically assume that all of the various proto-creeds or Christ hymns that are identified throughout the New Testament are gospel summaries for the reasons noted in the last chapter.[2] Beyond the creeds, hymns, trustworthy sayings and famous verses, there are then a number of biblical texts where the word 'gospel' itself is both used and, potentially, filled out. This is just small a subset of the many texts that use the word 'gospel' because, as we saw in the introduction, in most cases in the New Testament where the word is used, its meaning is assumed rather than expounded. But those texts where the word is both used and seemingly developed might give us the best chance of finding a direct presentation of the gospel in the New Testament, even if some of them do ultimately remain ambiguous on the question. The texts that we need to consider here are Mark 1:1, Mark 1:14–15, Acts 5:42, Romans 1:1–6, 2 Timothy 2:8 and 1 Corinthians 5:3b–5a.

Not without ambiguity

Mark 1:1

The opening chapter of Mark's Gospel offers two statements that might give us the gospel. The very first verse reads,

> The beginning of the good news [gospel] about Jesus the Messiah, the Son of God.
> (Mark 1:1)

Two critical questions immediately arise from this verse: what is the beginning of the good news, and what is the rest of the good news? Is the verse itself the beginning and the remainder of Mark's Gospel the rest? If this is correct, weight is given to the idea that the gospel message is captured by the entirety of Mark's Gospel, a view that we came across in the previous chapter. While it would be hard to dismiss this view outright, accepting verse 1 as something of a title and content statement for all of Mark in this way is not without its complexities.[3]

The first of these is that if *all* of Mark's Gospel is *the* gospel, then we need to decide if there is any legitimate way of summarising it down to something more easily communicable, or if anything less than all of Mark is less than the whole gospel. Assuming an accurate summary must be possible – because we would otherwise have to concede that few Christians know the whole gospel in its proper detail – we run back into the issue of determining which are the key events, motifs and themes and which can be deprioritised and left in the background. As we have seen, this will lead to diverse interpretations due to our subjective biases, and this is exactly what we find when we turn to different commentators' proposals for the core message of Mark's Gospel.[4] The problem is further multiplied when we bring the other written Gospels into our considerations. This is because all four Gospels have somewhat different emphases reflecting their somewhat different purposes, such that we can expect that each will be best summarised distinctly from the others, which leaves us with four somewhat different gospel summaries. Moreover, each of the written Gospels records a different set of events: there is partial, but not complete overlap between them. This means that if we do presume that each of the canonical Gospels communicates a common gospel, we might then need to conclude that the core of the gospel message can be ascertained apart from the contribution of every single event in every Gospel. The relationship between historical happenings and theology then comes into question again. It is all a complex, messy business that produces mixed results.

Before moving on though, there is an alternative way to understand Mark 1:1 that ought to be noted. It might be that, rather than this verse standing as an opening to all of Mark's Gospel, it more specifically leads into just the first thirteen or fifteen verses of the book or even just to the quotations of prophecies from Exodus, Malachi and Isaiah that immediately follow in verses 2 and 3.[5] If it primarily introduces these Old Testament references, then perhaps it is these that can helpfully be understood as the 'beginning of the gospel', a baseline from which the rest of Mark's message will progress. The prophecies are about the forerunner who would be sent to prepare the way of the Lord. Mark 1:4–8 tells us that those prophecies are fulfilled in John the Baptist, meaning in turn that the one to whom John points is the Lord.

On this understanding, Mark 1:1 says that the gospel message begins with the recognition that the Lord has come, and that he is Jesus the Messiah, the Son of God. This beginning would actually be an unexpected continuation of the Old Testament story from which arose the expectation of a great new king who would have earthly power, privilege and glory and who would act in the national, geopolitical and even military spheres like the great kings of old. But with this reading of the opening of Mark, the good news begins with the realisation that Jesus fulfils this role even if, to the human eye, he does not fit the bill in terms of his appearance, his situation or his conduct.

However, even if all of this is correct and grasped, it is still only a *beginning* point for understanding the gospel. Whatever the good news about Jesus is, it needs to be fleshed out *beyond* this beginning. Mark 1:1–3 tells us to start here, but not to stop here. Mark's 'beginning of the gospel' might therefore be more than a heading that introduces a narrative presentation of the gospel, it might be also the conceptual beginning point for our thinking and understanding of the gospel that must be filled out, developed and freshly reworked in light of the revelation of Jesus that the Gospel recounts. Either way, it is only a beginning, and we are still left to figure out what the rest of the gospel is.

Mark 1:14–15

Verses 14–15 of the same chapter of Mark can be dealt with far more straightforwardly. These record the beginning of Jesus' public ministry:

> After John was put in prison, Jesus went into Galilee, proclaiming the good news [gospel] of God. 'The time has come,' he said. 'The kingdom of God has come near. Repent and believe the good news [gospel]!'
> (Mark 1:14–15)

From this, it might be concluded that the gospel is the message that the time has come and the kingdom of God has come near, but a look at the original Greek text shows us that this is what Jesus declared *in addition* to the gospel. The passage actually says that he was proclaiming the gospel of God *and* (καὶ) saying these things.[6] If the fulfilment of time and nearness of the kingdom was the gospel message itself, the verses would essentially be saying

> After John was put in prison, Jesus went into Galilee, proclaiming that the time had come and the kingdom of God had come near, and saying, 'The time has come, and the kingdom of God has come near. Repent and believe that the time has come, and the kingdom of God has come near!'

There is no doubt that everything in these verses is intimately connected. The gospel is proclaimed because the time is fulfilled. Repentance and belief are also required because time has come. The kingdom of God has come near because the incarnate Christ has begun his proclamatory ministry. But dependency and close association does not mean that every phrase in the passage says precisely the same thing. The gospel can be inseparably related to yet technically distinct from the additional crucial things that Jesus is saying here about the immanence of the kingdom and the need for repentance and belief.

Acts 5:42

Another verse that seems to directly present the gospel is Acts 5:42, which says,

> Day after day, in the temple courts and from house to house, they [the apostles] never stopped teaching and proclaiming ['gospelling'] the good news that Jesus is the Messiah.
> (Acts 5:42)

Other English translations have 'Christ' instead of 'Messiah', and in place of 'is the' at the end of the verse, they have 'is' or 'as the', even though there are no words here at all in the original Greek.[7] A more literal (although far more clunky) translation of the second half of the verse would be 'they did not cease teaching and "gospelling" the Christ Jesus.' It is completely standard practice to presume the verb 'to be' and to add in the article where these are not given in Greek, and it is good and right to translate 'Christ' as 'Messiah'. However, by these choices, the translators make 'Messiah' the predicate of 'Jesus' and so have the apostles stating their gospel as the equation that Jesus is the Messiah of Israel.[8] This could be a fair translation, but 'gospelling the Christ Jesus' might also be less specific than 'to proclaim Jesus as the Messiah'. In fact, Acts 17:2–3 indicates that a fuller understanding of what it means to proclaim Christ Jesus involves speaking of his death and resurrection, not just his identity alone. Acts 5:42 is perhaps slightly more complicated than it seems at first.

Romans 1:1–6

For evangelical commentators, there seems to be no question that Romans 1:1–6 (or at least verses 1–4) contain a summary of the gospel message. Indeed, it is telling that this is usually not even argued for in the commentaries, but simply asserted as a self-evident fact.[9] These verses do use the term 'gospel' twice, and they also speak of the promise of the Old Testament Scriptures, the divine and human identity of Jesus, the personal nature of his lordship, his resurrection and the need for obedience towards him. However, even as we acknowledge that all of these matters are essential to our understanding of Christ and the Christian faith, we can still ask if Paul is bringing them together as any kind of systematic summary of the gospel message. A close reading of the text reveals that the gospel is *about* or *regarding* God's Son Jesus (verse 3), but verses 3–4 do not directly say what exactly it is about or regarding Jesus that constitutes the gospel message. They read,

> [Paul] set apart for the gospel of God – the gospel he promised beforehand through his prophets in the Holy Scriptures regarding his Son, who as to his earthly life was a descendant of David, and who through the Spirit of holiness was appointed the Son of God in power by his resurrection from the dead: Jesus Christ our Lord. (Romans 1:1–4)

The standard interpretation of these verses is that they reproduce one of the early Christian creeds outlining the content of the gospel message as being that God's Son was descended from David in his earthly life and appointed to be the Son of God by the Spirit's raising him from the dead.[10] There should be no doubt whatsoever that this is a declaration of true and important things about Jesus, here with a particular focus on his incarnation that encompasses both his royal human ancestry ('as to his earthly life was a descendant of David') and his divine parentage ('was appointed the Son of God'). But while the theology of the incarnation might be essential to the theological meaning of the gospel (as we will explore in chapter 5), it is not clear that it constitutes a full summary of the gospel in itself. For Romans 1:3–4 to present such a summary *unambiguously*, it would need to say something like

> [Paul] set apart for the gospel of God ... *which is that* as to his earthly life [he] was a descendant of David, and ... through the Spirit of holiness [he] was appointed the Son of God in power by his resurrection from the dead: Jesus Christ our Lord.

But the sentence is not written that way, and it seems better to read the text as having the primary purpose of filling out some essential detail of the identity of God's Son, Jesus Christ our Lord. The difference might be subtle, but it is significant. One way to show this, and to highlight the actual emphasis and content of the sentence, is to substitute the relevant contents of the passage for something more everyday while maintaining its primary syntax. An (indulgent) example of this would be

> [Tim] set apart for the good news ... regarding my mother, who as to her earthly life was a descendant of Marian, and who through the law of the land was made an Australian citizen ... Danusia our fellow image-bearer.

In focus here is my purpose as someone set aside for the communication of some good news that concerns a certain Danusia, whose identity can be understood and guaranteed in various ways, and which is here detailed as an expansion on her identification as my mother. It is not a natural reading to suggest that her identity is itself the good news. In fact, as we read this reworded passage, we do not think that the particular good news about her has been made clear at all yet; we only have the fact that there is some good news about this woman with this identity. In the same way, although Paul uses the word 'gospel' in the proper wording of verse 3, it is not unquestionably clear that he is either filling it out with the information he gives about Jesus' identity or making it his purpose to expound it systematically at all at this point. In fact, it could make more sense to see Paul's primary purpose in the opening words of Romans as being to establish his own authority as an apostle of the presently unexpounded message about Jesus, and as part of that, he takes the opportunity to insert the underlying authority of Jesus derived from his royal and divine identity. This is not unlike the openings of some of Paul's other letters (Galatians 1:1; Titus 1:1–3).

2 Timothy 2:8

Paul gives this directive in his second letter to Timothy:

> Remember Jesus Christ, raised from the dead, descended from David. This is my gospel.
> (2 Timothy 2:8)

Although this appears to be another direct and comprehensive assertion of the content of the gospel, the translation 'this is my gospel' is probably too strong. It would be better if that phrase were attached to the first sentence and rendered something like 'according to my gospel'. This would show that while the message of Christ raised from the dead is taken from the gospel, it might not be the wholeness of the gospel; there might be other truths that are also drawn out of the gospel and that also accord with it in the same way.[11] The wider context of this verse shows that it is another text where Paul's primary purpose is not to crystallise the gospel for his readers, but rather to offer some truths – quite possibly gospel-based truths, as well as his own life's example – as the basis for courage to persevere in the face of persecution.[12] Thus, to see how much of the gospel is captured in this verse, we would need to start with an even sharper text.

*

As we move to our last passage, we must once more remember that the reason for taking such a tight approach is that it ought to increase our confidence in our final findings even as, and precisely because, it limits the data we are admitting into the conversation. If we will only admit texts that pass a very high degree of scrutiny, then we can be all the more confident that those texts take us closer to the most accurate answer to our question. Additionally, we once more need to flag that we are not for a moment concluding that the texts we have considered above definitely do *not* present the gospel, only that without other evidence we cannot be fully certain that they do. Once we do have a firm concept of the gospel in mind, we can go back to some of these passages to see whether they do indeed offer us the gospel, whether they give us a part of the gospel, or if they are expressions of critical pieces of theology that are not the gospel themselves, but that they are somehow closely connected to the gospel. We are only temporarily putting these to the side as we search for a biblical text that unambiguously gives us a comprehensive gospel summary. Fortunately, there is one such text.

1 Corinthians 15:3b–5a

Unlike the texts explored above, 1 Corinthians 15:1–5 needs to be given priority not simply because it uses the word 'gospel', nor because it is sometimes recognised as another early Christian creed, nor because it just intuitively appears to contain key elements of the gospel. Rather, it demands attention because of its own direct claim that it is a summary of the apostolic gospel.

In verses 1–11, Paul is absolutely unambiguous in stating that what he is detailing here is the gospel. He makes this point in three ways, which actually come out best in relatively wooden translations of the original language, even if these sound a bit awkward to modern English readers. First, he states, 'I am making known to you, siblings, the gospel that I "gospelled" to you' (verse 1). Second, he says that this is information 'of first importance' and is that which he also received (verse 3), signalling not only its absolute priority, but also something of its historical recognition as gospel. Third, he says, 'Thus we proclaim' (verse 11), showing that his is the same message that is shared by the apostles and other witnesses to the resurrection. There can be little doubt that, as far as Paul is concerned, what he writes in verses 3b–5a is a clear summary of the authentic Christian gospel. There really is no alternative understanding, and this is exactly what we have been looking for. From this text, we read that the gospel is

> that Christ died for our sins in accordance with the Scriptures, and that he was buried, and that he has been raised on the third day in accordance with the Scriptures, and that he appeared
> (1 Corinthians 15:3b–5a, my translation)

We must acknowledge that this is not a fresh discovery in any way. Any commentator looking at these verses will acknowledge that this is a good expression of the New Testament's gospel, even if they have done that only intuitively or because the text is so widely recognised as such. However, not everyone lays so much weight upon the text as the single most dependable articulation of the gospel in the Bible to the exclusion of those that we have reviewed above, and not everyone will go on to analyse the verses in the same way. As it happens, a good interpretation of this text requires a recognition of its very deliberate structure.

The verses present four distinct statements, each introduced by 'that' or 'and that', which can lead to it being mapped out as follows:

> [The gospel is]
> *that* Christ died for our sins in accordance with the Scriptures,
> *and that* he was buried,
> *and that* he has been raised on the third day in accordance with the Scriptures,
> *and that* he appeared[13]

This might suggest that the gospel can be summarised into four primary points: the death, burial, resurrection and appearances of Christ. However, it makes good sense to take the first and third lines, which are each modified with 'in accordance with the Scriptures', as being primary, with the second and fourth lines subordinately relating to them. This is because the second and fourth lines both function to offer a piece of forensic evidence in support of the claims made in the first and third lines respectively. That is, the statement that Christ was buried presents the material evidence for the assertion that he died, and the statement that he appeared presents the eyewitness testimony for him having been raised again. Given this, it might be more helpful to lay the verses out so their grammatic and theological structures are both clearer, as follows:

[The gospel is]
that Christ died for our sins
in accordance with the Scriptures,
and that he was buried,
and
that he has been raised on the third day
in accordance with the Scriptures,
and that he appeared[14]

Now, we see more easily the very neat division of the gospel message into two parts, each capturing one event. The first event of the gospel is that Christ died for our sins, and the second is that he has been raised on the third day. With this layout, we can also see the directly parallel presentations of the attendant points made in relation to each of these two parts: their common alignment with the Old Testament Scriptures and the strong evidence supporting each claim. We can annotate our text thus:

[The gospel is]
that Christ died for our sins – *1st part of the gospel*
in accordance with the Scriptures, – *Fulfilling the OT*
and that he was buried, – *There was evidence*
and
that he has been raised on the third day – *2nd part of the gospel*
in accordance with the Scriptures, – *Fulfilling the OT*
and that he appeared – *There was evidence*

We learn several important things about the gospel when we see the text laid out in this way:

1. *Both* the death *and* resurrection of Christ are *co-central* in the gospel, something that evangelicals have sometimes struggled to capture. Therefore, any presentation of the *full* gospel cannot foreground the event of the cross at the expense of the resurrection, nor the event of the resurrection at the expense of the cross. They are equally important, and while inseparably related, neither one can be made completely derivative of the other.
2. We anticipate that the *theological meaning of the cross* will not be subsumed into the meaning of the resurrection, and that the *theological meaning of the resurrection* will not be subsumed into the meaning of the cross. They are distinct events for which we expect distinct meanings, and even if those meanings have deep and necessary connections, they are complementary to each other as much as they merely point to each other.
3. This presentation of the gospel shows that the greater story of the Scriptures is the backdrop to each of the two gospel events and should be included when expounding the gospel, but the wider Scriptures, the narratives they trace out and the doctrines they contain are not themselves part of the gospel proper. The death and resurrection of Christ were *in accordance with* the Scriptures, but the Old Testament Scriptures are not in and of themselves part of the gospel message.
4. This summary shows that while the gospel is about Christ (and in fact completely depends on his identity as the divine-human Messiah of Israel, as we will see in chapter 5), the gospel cannot be reduced to only his identity as King and Lord in a static sense, nor to his life story generally. Rather, it must be focused on the two specific events of his death and resurrection. The gospel is about the things that Christ has done, or that have been done for him. It is not just the bare fact that Jesus is the Christ.
5. We do not need to explain the burial and appearances of Christ as though they had the same fundamental significance as his death and resurrection. The burial of Christ is important, but what it

achieved was not of the same nature or magnitude as his death.[15] Similarly, the appearances of the risen Christ were critical to the hope and testimony of the early church, but they did not achieve anything of the same nature or magnitude as the resurrection itself. This is all another way of saying that we do not expect his burial or appearances to be freighted with the same theology as his death and resurrection.

6 Finally, this understanding of the gospel means that while we respect the importance of the narrative form of the Bible as we seek to interpret it, we must accept that the gospel can be properly summarised into these two propositions with their supporting statements, even as we recognise that those propositions are drawn from the passion and exaltation narratives. That is, we can and should embrace a propositional summary of the gospel; Paul's way of expressing the gospel is surely one that we can be happy with.[16]

In short, the gospel as presented by Paul in 1 Corinthians 15 is the message of the death and resurrection of the Christ. To be sure, the events of this message are narrated in the canonical Gospels, lie in the continuum of the entire Bible story and get unpacked and explained in many different parts of the New Testament. But the central message most simply stated is that Christ died for our sins and was raised on the third day. While not at all a novel claim, it is the case that this presentation of the gospel stands in contrast to those alternatives, which can include fewer or more events (for example, Christ's death only, or all of Christ's birth, miracles, death, burial, resurrection and ascension), or those that do not focus on any events at all and instead just point to the identity of Jesus as Lord. More positively, Paul's articulation of the gospel shows us that there is some truth and accuracy to all of the gospel proposals from the evangelical camp, which were surveyed in the last chapter. The gospel indeed centres on the cross, even if it has a *dual* focus on the cross *and* resurrection. The theology of the gospel is deeply eschatological, as the resurrection of Christ is the paradigmatic eschatological event, yet it will also have other theological emphases that arise from Christ's death and identity. And the gospel is all about the messiahship and lordship of Christ, although that is not a static identity but rather what makes the events of his death and resurrection effective and meaningful and is itself made meaningful by them.

In the next chapter, we will spend time considering the two events of the gospel in more detail, thinking about what actually happened when the divine-man Christ died and what his resurrection did and did not entail. In chapter 4, we will then proceed to consider the underlying theological meaning of the two events and see that it cannot be reduced to one of soteriology or eschatology, but must account for both of these in an integrated manner. In chapter 5, we will consider how his identity as Messiah is both worked out through these events and at the same time is absolutely essential for the events to be meaningful – that is, we will see the paramount importance of Christology in our unpacking of the gospel.

Wider soundings

Before proceeding, however, we can now briefly turn to see that Paul's gospel is the same gospel that is shot through the New Testament, even if the different texts in which we find it were not all written with the intention of outlining it systematically. There is a common gospel framework and even world-view within which all of the New Testament writers think, and this is easy to see when we highlight references to the two events of Jesus' death and resurrection, and his identity as Christ or Messiah, in a selection of passages taken from across the New Testament corpus.

Some of these are go-to gospel texts, including some that we have looked at above. Others are texts where we might not previously have seen the gospel. The texts below are just a small sampling to make the point, and in no way an exhaustive list of gospel references in the New Testament.

> From that time on Jesus [*Christ*] began to explain to his disciples that he must go to Jerusalem and suffer many things at the hands of the elders, the chief priests and the teachers of the law, and that he must be killed [*death*] and on the third day be raised to life [*resurrection*].
> (Matthew 16:21)[17]

Then he opened their minds so they could understand the Scriptures. He told them, 'This is what is written: the Messiah [*Christ*] will suffer [*death*] and rise from the dead on the third day [*resurrection*].'
(Luke 24:45–46)

Just as Moses lifted up the snake in the wilderness, so the Son of Man [*Christ*] must be lifted up [on the cross: *death*], that everyone who believes may have eternal life in him [*resurrection*].
(John 3:14–15)

For God so loved the world that he gave [over to *death*] his one and only Son [*Christ*], that whoever believes in him shall not perish but have eternal life [*resurrection*].
(John 3:16)

This man [*Christ*] was handed over to you by God's deliberate plan and foreknowledge; and you, with the help of wicked men, put him to *death* by nailing him to the cross. But God raised him from the dead [*resurrection*], freeing him from the agony of *death*, because it was impossible for *death* to keep its hold on him.
(Acts 2:23–24)

Therefore let all Israel be assured of this: God [through *resurrection* (verse 32)] has made this Jesus, whom you crucified [*death*], both Lord and Messiah [*Christ*].
(Acts 2:36)

As was his custom, Paul went into the synagogue, and on three Sabbath days he reasoned with them from the Scriptures, explaining and proving that the Messiah [*Christ*] had to suffer [*death*] and rise from the dead [*resurrection*]. 'This Jesus I am proclaiming to you is the Messiah [*Christ*],' he said.
(Acts 17:2–3)

But God has helped me to this very day; so I stand here and testify to small and great alike. I am saying nothing beyond what the prophets

> and Moses said would happen – that the Messiah [*Christ*] would suffer [*death*] and, as the first to rise from the dead [*resurrection*], would bring the message of light to his own people and to the Gentiles.
> (Acts 26:22–23)

> For if, while we were God's enemies, we were reconciled to him through the *death* of his Son [*Christ*], how much more, having been reconciled, shall we be saved through his life [*resurrection*]!
> (Romans 5:10)

> Remember Jesus *Christ*, raised [*resurrection*] from the dead [*death*], descended from David. This is my gospel.
> (2 Timothy 2:8)

> But when this priest [*Christ*] had offered for all time one sacrifice for sins [*death*], he sat down at the right hand of God [having been *resurrected*].
> (Hebrews 10:12)

> For *Christ* also suffered once for sins [*death*], the righteous for the unrighteous, to bring you to God. He was put to *death* in the body but made alive [*resurrection*] in the Spirit.
> (1 Peter 3:18)

> When I saw him, I fell at his feet as though dead. Then he placed his right hand on me and said: 'Do not be afraid. I am the First and the Last [*Christ*]. I am the Living One; I was dead [*death*], and now look, I am alive for ever and ever [*resurrection*]! And I hold the keys of death and Hades.'
> (Revelation 1:17–18)

Finally, we can even note that when we have these eyes to see, we do in fact find the core elements of the gospel reflected even in Galatians 1:

> Grace and peace to you from God our Father and the Lord Jesus *Christ*, who gave himself for our sins [*death*] to rescue us from the

present evil age [through *resurrection*], according to the will of our God and Father, to whom be glory for ever and ever. Amen.
(Galatians 1:3–5)

3
What actually happened: the two gospel events

Having arrived at a solid definition of the gospel proper, we now come to consider what actually happened in its two central events: the death and resurrection of Christ. Initially, there might be a sense that there is little to explore here as the facts, if accepted, are straightforward enough: Jesus died, and then he was restored back to life. However, it does not take much reflection to realise that these simple assertions refer to happenings that are in many ways complicated to understand. For example, what do we actually think happened when the Son of God, the Second Person of the Holy Trinity, died? Did he cease to exist? Is that even possible for one of the persons of God? If we decide that it is not plausible, then do we start thinking that Christ did not really or completely die after all? Did some part of him always remain alive in some way? Of course, if we go this way, we run into other problematic questions, such as whether or not Christ was genuinely, fully human and whether there can be any real benefits from his going through only some kind of semi- or pseudo-death.

Moving on to think about his resurrection, do we, on the one hand, believe that it was not a return to full, embodied life, but something more ghostly or phantom-like? If so, what would this mean for our own resurrection hope? Would we then become ghosts like those we know from films and cartoons? On the other hand, if we believe that resurrection is simply a return to life as it is before death, does that mean that the Christian hope is just for more of the same with no difference except that we will be invulnerable? Also, given that the Bible records many instances of people returning to life after death, why is Christ's resurrection deemed to be so significant? Is it not just another example of a recognised phenomenon, albeit a rare one? All of these matters need some attention, but our first task is to think briefly about the dying of Christ as something distinct from his death.

The crucifixion of Christ

The statements 'Jesus died' and 'Jesus died on the cross' might appear at first to be essentially equivalent, with the second simply expanding the first to detail the place where the death happened. On one level, this is right, but on another, the *fact* of Jesus' death and the *manner* of his death are two quite different things, and quite different theological significance is attached to each. To put it another way, if it is only the fact of Jesus' death that is significant, and the means by which he died was largely irrelevant or incidental to the fact, then there would be no real reason that Jesus should not have died in a battle, or in a back alley, or indeed quietly and peacefully in his sleep. But the New Testament repeatedly makes very clear that Jesus died *on a cross*, and it even gives us some of the attendant circumstances of that particular way of death. There seems no way that this can be of incidental importance.

Martin Hengel's classic work *Crucifixion* unpacks in some detail everything that Roman crucifixion entailed – from its quite terrifyingly gruesome mechanics, to its public nature, to its use as a punishment for only the lowest members of society.[1] In sum, Hengel helps us to see that crucifixion is among the most tortuous modes of execution ever devised, and that it was intended to be a stark public deterrent, as those condemned were hung out in open view for the duration of their suffering, and then even left there after they had expired such that their bodies might begin to decay or be picked at by feral animals. Unlike the more regulated versions of capital punishment that still exist in some countries today – lethal injection, electrocution or firing squad, for example – there is no attempt to limit the period of suffering in crucifixion, nor to offer any measures that preserve the victim's dignity. Death by crucifixion was meant to inflict and prolong as much physical agony as possible and to be completely and utterly degrading.

In addition to delivering this physical agony and public humiliation, crucifixion was also meant to identify its victim as one of the lowest, most offensive and abhorrent members of society; someone who could be seen as deserving of such an end. Perhaps today, we would want to place people such as genocidal dictators and serial paedophiles in that group, but in the first-century Roman world, it included those convicted of treason. Threatening the stability of the empire was intolerable and so attracted not just the harshest of all punishments but also the broadest, most utter ruining of reputation. Moreover, because crucifixion was largely reserved for slaves and non-citizens, those who were killed in this way were considered to be of fundamentally less value to begin with. Thus, Jesus did not only die by state execution; he also died with crowds watching him suffer incomparable and excruciating (a word derived from 'crucifixion') pain throughout his entire naked and brutalised body for hours on end, all the while reckoning that he was a relatively worthless being whose crimes must have warranted his end. For many, this would undermine all possibility of there being anything good or worthy in his person, message or mission. Plus, for those who might still have held onto some belief in his cause, the fear of facing a similar fate would have given them pause to consider whether it was worth the risk to act on those convictions.

Next, the obvious fact that Christ's death sentence was unjust must be remembered. According to the biblical witness, Jesus was unambiguously innocent of the crimes for which he was tried and sentenced (for example, Luke 22:66–23:25). The Jewish leadership he confronted was too narrow-minded and protective of their own privilege to accept Jesus' radical words and so, not themselves having the right to execute anyone while under the jurisdiction of Rome yet knowing that the occupiers would not sentence anyone to death for breaking Jewish law, they presented him to the Roman authorities as a political rebel (for example, Luke 23:2). Their suggestion that they were pursuing the interests of their oppressors in this matter was as disingenuous as their charges were false. For any who would look objectively into Jesus' words and actions, it is clear that he had not been making any claims that rejected the Jewish Scriptures, and that had he not been rallying a militia to rise up in opposition to Caesar or the Romans either. But where the Jews were protective of their own privilege, the Romans were happy to settle for appeasement rather than seek out proper justice. Thus, they sentenced Jesus to death in circumstances that mean he must be numbered among the world's most unjustly treated.

Finally, for Jews, crucifixion also had a weighty theological dimension. Deuteronomy 21:22–23 teaches that anyone left hanging on a tree as a form of judicial execution is cursed by God. If the cross is equivalent to a tree, as Acts 13:29 and Galatians 3:13 indicate, then on top of everything else, in his death, Jesus was also seen to be placed under God's wrath.[2] He was marked as God's enemy, not his representative. This would only have reinforced the deterrent effect of his death for any Jewish people who witnessed it.

Nowadays, the cross is universally recognised as being the sign of the Christian faith, which, at its best, is a faith expressed in peace and love, even if it often can seem old fashioned, stuffy and institutionalised. Of course, at various times, cross designs have also found their way out of Christianity and into mainstream fashion and jewellery. But the cross should be a reminder of a truly horrific death, and it should make us wince as much as smile when we see it. To the person who does not understand the achievements of Christ's death, the adoption of the symbol of the cross by the church should be as shocking as if the civil rights movement chose a hunting rifle as its logo to commemorate the work of Dr Martin Luther King Jr, except that even death by a sniper's shot does not have all of the connotations of death by crucifixion as sketched above. Christ's death on the cross carries a lot of specific meaning beyond the bare fact that it happened to be how he was killed and beyond it being a state-authorised execution. In the crucifixion, Jesus was in no way distanced or insulated from any of the intense pain, humiliation, degradation, injustice or cursings of the world. Instead, he was taking them all onto himself, bearing them in his body and, as we will see in the next chapter, this has a significant bearing on the meaning of the event of his death.

Can God really die?

As pre-empted above, the very idea that Christ as true God could and did die is difficult to integrate into any fuller orthodox understanding of God, and it potentially has some frightening implications. If there was a way that the Son could really die, albeit via the path of incarnation, is there any way that the Father and the Holy Spirit could also die? Could God will himself entirely out of existence, and if so, where does that leave us? On one level, this is a silly question akin to a child asking if God could create a rock so heavy that even he could not lift it. But it is not entirely frivolous given that, according to the gospel, one person of the Trinity *did* die at a moment in recorded history. And even if we decide that we cannot admit the possibility of the Father and Spirit also dying at any point, we are still left with the matter of what was going on in the Trinity for the period when Christ was dead. Was there a temporary 'Binity' of just two persons of the Godhead? Of course, the problem with this speculation is that it could lead us to think that his Trinitarian nature is somehow incidental to God; it might be how he usually chooses to exist, but it is not completely fundamental to him. If we go down this path, we quickly find that we are talking about a different God than the one we meet in the Scriptures, as we have no biblical grounds on which to posit a God whose essential nature could change like this.

Tapping into related questions, Jürgen Moltmann, in his famous *The Crucified God*, draws attention to the fact that, in the death of Jesus,

> The Fatherlessness of the Son is matched by the Sonlessness of the Father, and if God has constituted himself as the Father of Jesus Christ, then he also suffers the death of his Fatherhood in the death of the Son.[3]

Moltmann's primary concern here is the suffering of the Father as part of the Trinitarian experience of the Son's death, but the idea that in Christ's death the Father ceases to be Father, even temporarily, is confronting. It again suggests the possibility of fundamental changes to the nature and the persons of God, and it highlights the fact that there can be complete relational loss within the Trinity, something that could lead to further disturbing questions about the durability of the intra-Trinitarian bonds of love.

Kenotic theory, developed from certain interpretations of Philippians 2:7, can lead to somewhat similar places. Some versions of it claim that what Christ emptied (Greek: ekenōsen) himself of in his incarnation was a portion of his divinity, allowing such things as his ignorance of some of the Father's plans, as well as his mortality.[4] The problem is once more the impact that this has on the unity of the Trinity, as well as the way that it dilutes Christ's divinity. Against this idea, classical orthodox theology would say that rather than losing anything through the incarnation, when the Word became flesh, he took on more – in particular the fullness of humanity – all the while retaining the fullness of his divine nature. In this framing, the emptying of Philippians 2 is probably better understood as Jesus voluntarily giving up his exalted position, rather than losing any of his divine attributes.

Centuries before Moltmann and Kenotic theory, and perhaps wary of some of the issues that such views could run into, John Calvin came at Christ's death from the opposite direction. In his *Institutes of the Christian Religion*, he says,

> The Son of God descended miraculously from heaven, yet without abandoning heaven; was pleased to be conceived miraculously in the Virgin's womb, to live on the earth, and hang upon the cross, and yet always filled the world as from the beginning.[5]

Reinforcing the classical and orthodox view, Calvin maintains that the fullness of God was in Christ as he entered, dwelled and died among humanity. And yet, at the same time, Christ is held to have simultaneously existed in an extra, parallel, heavenly mode or experience, just as he always had done. This belief is now commonly named for Calvin – the *extra Calvinisticum* – and it is helpfully associated with another that comes in the very next section of the *Institutes*: the *communicatio idiomatum* or 'communication of properties'. The *communicatio* captures the fact that the Scriptures

> sometimes attribute to him [Christ] qualities which should be referred specially to his humanity, and sometimes qualities applicable peculiarly to his divinity, and sometimes qualities which embrace both natures, and do not apply specially to either. This combination of a twofold nature in Christ they express so carefully, that they sometimes communicate them with each other.[6]

This doctrine explains that while the Bible speaks of the Son of God, say, being seen, weeping or dying, it is then technically referring to experiences of his human nature but allowing them to be spoken about as though they were true of his whole divine-human person generally. His humanity is 'communicated', or pragmatically applied, to his divinity. Similarly, when relating things like Christ performing miracles, which strictly speaking are acts of his divine nature, the Bible can attribute them to his whole person generally. This way of thinking is grounded in the fact that there is such an essential connection between Christ's two natures that the attributes or actions properly associated with one can be 'transferred improperly, but not causelessly' – that is, with a justifiable rationale – to the other.[7]

Together, the *extra Calvinisticum* and the *communicatio idiomatum* are important because the former protects the integrity of Trinity while the latter accounts for the capacity of the Son as a real human to do and experience things that cannot be experienced by God as he is known throughout the Scriptures and vice versa. In this conceptualisation, Christ can be a real human who truly dies without compromising his divinity, nor the Father's father-ness, nor any other aspect of the nature of the Trinity. This is because the *extra Calvinisticum* allows us to say that it was Christ in his earthly existence that died, not Christ in his heavenly mode, and the *communicatio idiomatum* says that even as this is technically so, we are free to speak of the complete Son of God dying because his two natures are completely inseparable such that what we say of one, we can reasonably speak of as being true for the other.

As useful as these theological devices might be, they are rather complicated and might not solve as many problems as they appear to at first. It can be fairly asked whether the idea of Christ existing in two parallel 'modes' in some ways weakens orthodox Christology, which, according to the benchmark formula of the AD 451 Council of Chalcedon, recognises the two natures of Christ 'without division, without separation'.[8] We can certainly see some irony in the fact that the *communicatio idiomatum* enables us to avoid needing to think about Christ existing in two modes, while the *extra Calvinisticum* makes a point of asserting that we should do this very thing. Can we have our cake and eat it too? In all of this, we see that even the great theologians have found that thinking about how Christ could possibly die is not at all straightforward. Fortunately however, there might be a completely different way to move forward in our understanding of the death of Jesus.

The nature of death

In addition to starting our thinking about Christ's death through the lens of his divinity as we have done so far, it can also prove fruitful to consider the nature of his death as a human being. That is, we can take a bottom-up as well as a top-down approach. As we do this, it is most important to begin by clearing away a common assumption about what happens when a human being dies that does not line up with what the Bible teaches. That assumption is that upon dying, humans cease to exist. Something like this would seem to be in the background of Moltmann's thoughts about the death of Christ resulting in the painful end of intra-Trinitarian relationships, as this only makes sense with the belief that, at some level, Christ ceased to exist as the divine Son between his death and resurrection. Conversely, Calvin's view seems well-designed to protect against any notion that the Son could cease to exist: if his heavenly mode is never subject to death, then there is no risk of this even when his human body dies.

Throughout the history of the church, there have been defenders of the various expressions of Christian mortalism, which are doctrinal positions about the non-existence of human beings after their death, but these have never been the mainstream position of the church, as it is not clear that they best capture the witness of Scripture.[9] Rather than presenting death as the moment at which a human ceases to exist, the biblical evidence instead points towards it being a tearing apart of the human body and soul, or spirit, both of which then continue to exist, even if in very different states. The evil of death is not that it leads into nothingness, but rather that it literally rips apart and disintegrates the whole human person. Fundamentally, humans are body and soul or spirit. In death, this fundamental oneness is destroyed, as these are horrifically split.

It is necessary to make a short aside here to consider whether it is biblically correct to think of body and soul as the two constituent parts of a human being, contra flesh and spirit, a tripartite division such as spirit, soul and body, or even something more complex like a blend of heart, soul, mind and strength.[10] Alternatively, some might completely object to the idea of humans being made up of distinct aspects at all, seeing that as a more dualistic Platonic than Christian idea and so representing an intrusion of Greek philosophy into biblical theology. These people might argue that when Scripture uses different terms to discuss the different dimensions of human beings, it is doing so as a rhetorical means of addressing our inclinations and dispositions, not to describe our ontology, and certainly there is something right about this. Furthermore, there is something to be said for the idea that humans do not *have* distinct bodies and souls in the way that we have our various possessions, but instead that we *are* our bodies and souls. There is no way to meaningfully conceive of a person apart from either of them. A bodiless human is as meaningless as an immaterial solid object. A soulless human is subhuman at best. But even as we recognise the validity in all of these questions and viewpoints, it nonetheless remains the case that the Bible often uses body and soul language for human beings, and it presents many examples of the separation of body and soul in death. Examples of this post-mortem division of a person include the medium of Endor bringing up the (presumably) disembodied soul of the deceased Samuel at Saul's request (1 Samuel 28:3–20), Paul's desire to depart from his body and be with Christ (2 Corinthians 5:6–9; Philippians 1:20–26), the return of souls from heaven and the raising of dead bodies at the second coming of Christ (1 Thessalonians 4:13–18), and the souls of martyrs crying out to God from under the heavenly altar as they long for the coming day of judgement (Revelation 6:9–11, cf. Revelation 20:4).

It is true that there are texts in the Bible that speak of the destruction of the body, but it is important to recognise that these neither immediately nor necessarily connect that to death. Two parallel passages from the Gospels are instructive here. In Luke 12, Jesus says,

> I tell you, my friends, do not be afraid of those who kill the body and after that can do no more. But I will show you whom you should fear: fear him who, after your body has been killed, has authority to throw you into hell. Yes, I tell you, fear him.
> (Luke 12:4–5)

And in Matthew 10, he says,

> Do not be afraid of those who kill the body but cannot kill the soul. Rather, be afraid of the One who can destroy both soul and body in hell.
> (Matthew 10:28, cf. Revelation 21:8)

Together, these texts draw distinctions between killing the body and killing the soul, and between killing bodies and souls and the later condemnation to and destruction in hell. The difference between killing the body and killing the soul is admittedly hard to understand, but what is clear from these verses is that death is not a person's end; it is rather followed by subsequent experiences that might or might not include the destruction of both body and soul in hell.

It could be interjected here that that we can and indeed do observe the decay of human bodies through physical processes that occur in our temporal realm: dead bodies decompose before reaching hell. Likewise, bodies can be burned up in cremation or otherwise dispersed, such that they no longer meaningfully exist. Once again, we note that this does not always happen at the instant of death, but is often subsequent to it. Most often, after death, a lifeless body is left behind. It does not immediately cease to exist. In addition, it is also not at all clear that there is any parallel process of natural decay that occurs for disembodied souls. In short, death and ceasing to exist are not the same thing, and if there is a final destruction of body or soul, that tends to come at some point after death.

Given that the Chalcedonian Definition includes a summary of the Bible's teaching that Christ was

> complete in manhood [*sic passim*] … truly man, consisting also of a reasonable soul and body … of one substance with us as regards his manhood; like us in all respects, apart from sin,

we have every reason to believe that his death was the same as any human death: it was the ripping apart of his body and soul.[11]

Although this might seem at first like a reversal of his incarnation, something that would introduce its own theological conundrums, it is not. Rather, it is an experience only made possible by the incarnation, as without a body or soul – both attributes of his humanity according to Chalcedon – Christ could not go through the process of death. One reason that Christ took on flesh was precisely so he could die a death like every other human death.

The great benefit of thinking about Christ's death in this way is that it allows us to see it as a very real death, as real as every other human death and yet not leading to a state of non-existence that creates all of the Trinitarian complications that the theologians wrestle with. Of course, we plainly see the truth of Christ's body and soul being separated in the fact that Christ's lifeless body continued to exist after his death, with the Gospels recording it being pierced, taken off the cross, embalmed and placed in the tomb (for example, John 19:31–42). So too we understand that his soul or spirit continued on. Luke 23:46 records Jesus crying out in a loud voice and saying, 'Father, into your hands I commit my spirit,' immediately before his last breath. This might be no more than an idiom, but perhaps there is more to it, especially if we couple it with the idea that after his death Christ's soul or spirit proceeded to 'paradise' with that of the criminal who had died on the neighbouring cross (Luke 23:40–43).

So while it is not unimportant to think about Christ's death in terms of the implications for his divine nature, coming to it from his true humanity might be less complicated to understand, and might in fact resolve some of the more difficult issues. If his death was the separation of his body and soul like every other human death, then there is no need to worry about the non-existence of God scenario, nor to resort to the idea of the Son having two parallel modes of existence. His death is not him being extinguished; it is him suffering the dreadful pulling apart of that which ought never to be divided. He suffers the horror that every human has faced since the fall. And again, we really must understand this severing of body and soul as a truly terrible fate. There is no sense in the Bible that death is not so bad because it is not a complete cessation of existence. Rather, the Scriptures present the separation of bodies and souls as a profoundly traumatic distortion, disordering and disintegration. While it is possible for people to be sheared apart in this way, this is no freeing of the entrapped soul as it is sometimes imagined in alternate spiritualities or philosophies. Rather, it is a deeply wrong and distressing state, and it screams out for healing, reversal, restoration and some assurance that it will never happen again. Ultimately, it screams out for resurrection.

Resurrection: beginning the new while continuing the old

Most wings of the Christian church are straightforward in their proclamation of the resurrection of Jesus. After all, in near-identical wording, each of the three ecumenical creeds – the Apostles', Nicene and Athanasian – declare that on the third day he rose again from the dead. Despite this, in recent generations there has been some dissent from more liberal theologians who have sought to explain away the biblical accounts of everything miraculous in an attempt to show a post-Enlightenment world that faith in God does not require a suspension of belief in the inviolability of the laws of nature. In this context, the resurrection accounts can only be palatable if taken as metaphors or if understood not literally but 'spiritually', whatever that might mean in that conversation. From here arise ideas such as 'the cause of Christ living on in our hearts' being offered as the true meaning of the resurrection and appealing both to more mystically inclined religious devotees as well as to more rigid adherents of scientism.[12] Plenty of retorts to these kinds of novel interpretations have been voiced by Christian apologists over the years, and the firm commitment to the plain fact of Jesus' resurrection as a touchstone of the faith remains strong in Bible-believing circles.[13] The belief is not going anywhere in a hurry.

More positively, however, historians of recent years have also contended that the literal resurrection of Christ is not only a sufficient cause of the rise of the Christian movement in its first few centuries, but even a necessary one.[14] According to their research, there is no other phenomenon than a person witnessed to have been raised from the dead that could explain how a small and powerless offshoot of the relatively minor Jewish religion could have come to dominate the Roman Empire by the early 300s. Jesus must have risen, or the church would not exist. But even when this history has been well-presented, much of the more popular effort has still been put towards demonstrating the fact that Christ's resurrection is something *that happened* rather than on explaining much about exactly *what happened*, with the common assertion being that his resurrection simply meant a revival of his physical body. This is correct but also quite inadequate. To more fully comprehend the event of Christ's resurrection in its fullness, we need to understand it as not only a return back to life but also as a restoration, a reunion and, importantly, a transformation.

Restoration and reunion

In the final ninety-second scene of Mel Gibson's two-hour-plus film *The Passion of the Christ*, the resurrected Jesus stands up in his tomb, ready to re-emerge to the surprise of his followers and the world outside. What is most visually striking about this closing moment is not that the Christ is alive again – most viewers would not have been shocked to learn that the story ended in this way – but that, apart from the nail hole visible in his hand, Jesus' body is clean, and his skin is flawlessly intact. This is in stark contrast to how he appeared in the scene immediately before, when his body was removed from the cross. There, he was filthy and grimy, bloodied all over and severely lacerated, a result of the ruthless flogging that the Gospels mention only briefly but that the film shows at some length and in gruesome detail.[15] There is no direct biblical confirmation that Jesus' body was healed in this way, although we do know that he retains the puncture wounds inflicted during his execution (John 20:24–29). Even so, we can at least say that the material damage that resulted in his mortal life's final ending was reversed. In his resurrection, he experienced some kind of significant physical healing and restoration of his flesh. His heart started to beat again, his lungs started taking in air once more and blood returned to flowing as it should. Death and its immediate material causes were undone.

Evangelicals are fond of quoting the spiritual truth 'by his wounds we are healed' from Isaiah 53:5 as a way of pointing to the forgiveness of sins secured by Jesus' death, but they perhaps less frequently remember that in his resurrection, he himself was physically restored too. First of all then, Jesus' resurrection involved a mending of his body. As an aside, it is worth noting here that the miraculous healings recorded in the Bible are similarly all acts of restoration and, as such, are meant to point forward to the ultimate restoration of resurrection.

In addition to this physical healing, or perhaps as part of it, Christ's resurrection obviously also involved the reunion of his body and soul or spirit, and given what we have already said about the nature of human death, this is exactly what we expect from resurrection. The tearing apart of body and soul can only be remedied by their reunification. We do not know exactly how this happened. None of the Gospels present the actual moment of Christ's resurrection, presumably because it occurred within the sealed tomb without any witnesses present, and because there is no record of Jesus ever having discussed the mechanics of it. All we have in the New Testament is evidence of Jesus' post-resurrection appearances which, as we recall from Paul's articulation of the gospel in 1 Corinthians 15, are the critical proof of his return to embodied life. Neither is there an abundance of biblical texts that speak of the whereabouts of Christ's spirit between his death and resurrection while his body lay in the tomb. Some quarters have developed extensive and detailed views on this, perhaps most notably the Roman Catholic Church. They maintain that between his death and resurrection, Christ went and 'harrowed hell', that is, he liberated the faithful Old Testament believers from one of the outer tiers of hell where they had been waiting for him before he subsequently delivered them into heaven.[16] This understanding is based on a certain reading of texts such at 1 Peter 3:18–20, and it neatly cleaves together with the Roman Catholic doctrine of purgatory, which finds its greatest support in the apocryphal book of 2 Maccabees, but it is probably not the best interpretation of the passage.[17] At any rate, this is a tangential issue, as the point here is simply that Christ's resurrection involved the reunification of his body and spirit such that he could return to the sphere of embodied, animated, material life. In his resurrection, that which was broken by the horrific tearing into two was fixed and reunited back to its proper state as one.

Transformation

As central as these concepts of restoration and reunion are, they do not exhaust the total of what occurred in Christ's resurrection, not by some way. We must also recognise that Christ's resurrection was radically transformative. Something occurred in his resurrection that made him very different from how he was before he died. There are a number of reasons why this has often been overlooked in evangelical Christianity, but we will briefly note just two. The first is that during the Reformation, the Protestants emphasised that Christ was raised to his 'selfsame' body as a way of undercutting the Roman Catholic doctrine of transubstantiation – the belief that in Communion, the bread and wine become the real body and blood of Christ. The Protestant argument was that if Christ's resurrection body was exactly the same as his body prior to death, then there was no way that parts of it could be repeatedly conjured up in Catholic rituals because true human bodies cannot be in more than one place at one time.[18] In this presentation of resurrection, the fact of restoration is prioritised, and it is this emphasis that has been handed on to many subsequent generations of Protestant believers. The second reason that evangelicals tend not to think much about the transformation of resurrection is that they are committed to pushing back against those liberal speculations that Christ's resurrection needs to be taken metaphorically or in some abstract spiritual sense, as mentioned above. The conservative counter to this has largely rested upon the materiality of the resurrection and has shied away from the idea that there was anything new, mystical or spiritual in Jesus' resurrection. To explore those possibilities would risk ceding too much ground to the opposition. But when we put aside the need to play defence against assaults on the belief in bodily resurrection and turn to look at the whole of what the Scriptures say, the picture is somewhat fuller.

For starters, in the post-resurrection narratives of the Gospels, there are consistent indications that in both his appearances and his movements, Christ is unexpectedly different from how he was before he died.[19] Luke 24:13–35 presents Cleopas and his travelling companion's encounter with the risen Jesus on the way to Emmaus, and the text highlights that they fail completely to recognise him until he breaks bread with them at the evening meal. Moreover, as soon as they do recognise him, he vanishes from their sight, something that we have no record of him doing in his pre-death ministry. This incident is also referred to in the non-canonical, longer ending of Mark's Gospel, which intriguingly says that Jesus appeared 'in a different form' (Mark 16:12). Even if this cannot be taken as a biblical witness, it is still a very early (probably second-century) church understanding of Christ having a transformed body in his resurrection.[20]

In Luke 24:36–40, the disciples presume that the risen Jesus is a ghost, possibly because his appearance was somehow different from what it had been before. In John 20:11–18, we have the account of Mary meeting the risen Jesus outside the tomb, but again, 'she did not realise that it was Jesus' until he spoke her name. In John 20:19–20, the disciples do not rejoice that they have seen Jesus until after he has shown them hands and his side, presumably as proof that he was who his face did not reveal him to be.[21] Then, in both John 20:19 and 26, Jesus appears before his disciples, despite the fact that they were in rooms with locked doors. Like his disappearance after the Emmaus road meeting, this is not how the Gospels record Jesus moving from place to place prior to his resurrection. Something is different now. Finally, in John 21:1–14, we have Jesus on the shore of the Sea of Tiberius with his disciples unable to recognise him until he successfully predicts a huge haul of fish for them if they follow his instructions. Once they join him on the shore, John records that 'none of the disciples dared ask him, "Who are you?" They knew it was the Lord' (John 21:12). This is an odd comment to include in the narrative, unless there was fair reason to assume that, although now knowable, Jesus was still somehow perceived differently by the senses. Matthew's Gospel has a brief report of a resurrection appearance in its closing four verses. There, the disciples worship him, 'but some doubted' (Matthew 28:17). There is no explanation of what or why they doubt, but given what we have seen in the other Gospels, it is plausible that they have questions about the identity of Jesus owing to his different appearance.[22]

Of course, there could be alternative interpretations of what is happening in each of these interactions. Perhaps they occurred when it was dark, perhaps Jesus was wearing a hooded cloak or maybe he was standing far off. But the problem with these sorts of explanations is that we need one for almost every post-resurrection appearance of Jesus, and there is no evidence in the text for any of them. These are arguments from silence. It seems far better to accept that in his resurrection, Christ was somehow changed in his physicality, and this would seem especially likely given what the Apostle Paul writes about the nature of the resurrection body.

In 1 Corinthians 15, directly following Paul's summary of the gospel, we find the longest exposition of resurrection in the New Testament. In verses 35–55, Paul directly responds to the questions 'How are the dead raised? With what kind of body will they come?' (verse 35) by developing an answer that is absolutely emphatic that it is a *different* body from that which they had before.[23] He rallies a number of illustrations to make the point: the fact that different created things have different bodies each with a different 'splendour' (verses 38–41); that what is sown and what is raised do not have the same form (verses 42b–44); and that the image of Adam, a man 'of the dust of the earth', differs from that of Christ, 'the heavenly man', 'a life-giving spirit' (verses 45–49). In all of this, Paul is disavowing his readers of any notion that the resurrection body could really be 'selfsame' with the mortal body. Moreover, he is explicit that all believers must themselves also undergo the transformation that resurrection brings if they are to inherit the kingdom because part of the transformation involves putting on imperishability and immortality and so being freed from the sting of death (verses 50–55). Most interestingly, Paul says that even those who have not died at the time of Christ's return must go through this transformation (verses 52–53), underscoring that restoration and reunion are not the full extent of what resurrection achieves. If they were, then those who were alive and well at the time of the parousia would be set for their future without any change needed, but this is not the case. They must experience the same kind of transformation as those who will be raised from the dead.

Overall, 1 Corinthians 15 presents the change that accompanies resurrection as being from physical to spiritual, although it is important to note that this is an *additive* change rather than a substitution, perhaps a little like Christ taking on humanity in his incarnation rather than giving up any of his divinity. While the text speaks of dying physically and being raised spiritually (verse 44), that cannot mean that the physical body is replaced by one that is spiritual but not physical, as Christ was demonstrably physical in his resurrection. He ate meals, encouraged his disciples to touch him and remarked about visibly having flesh and bones (Luke 24:39; John 20:26–27, 21:12–13). What being raised spiritually means is that a person's resurrection transformation results in them being more completely expressive of pure spirituality in some way. This entails many things and is not solely a moral or attitudinal change, neither of which Christ needed. Rather, it is so comprehensive a change that it is even expressed physically, the gap between the physical and the spiritual not being as far or absolute as we might sometimes think. On one level then, the historical defenders of the 'sameness' of Christ's mortal body and his resurrection body are correct: there is complete continuity from one to the other, such that he still bears the major scars of his crucifixion in his risen body. But at the same time, there was radical change as Christ's resurrection made him something new: the first human fit for the new creation, indeed the firstfruits of the new creation in which the whole created order will be completely spiritual while still very much material.[24] This is a big idea, and we will need to say more about it in chapter 5. For now, we simply affirm that in his resurrection, Christ was transformed such that his still-physical body became even more purely spiritual, and this change somehow impacted his physicality.

Before moving on, we must briefly address the question of whether or not Christ really was the first person to be resurrected, and whether or not his resurrection was a particularly unique event. This is because, as we noted at the start of this chapter, there are many other biblical accounts of people being raised from the dead before him. Examples include the boys raised by Elijah and Elisha (1 Kings 17:17–24; 2 Kings 4:32–37); those whom Jesus himself raised: the widow's son at Nain (Luke 7:11–17), Jairus' daughter (Mark 5:21–24, 35–43) and Lazarus (John 11:1–44); the multitude who came out of the tombs when Christ died on the cross (Matthew 27:52–53); Peter's raising of Tabitha (Acts 9:36–42); and Paul's raising of Eutychus (Acts 20:7–12). Given all of these and the others that could also be cited, it might be asked why Christ's resurrection is so significant. It is the understanding of resurrection as not only restoration of life and reunion of body with soul but also as transformation that gives the answer. None of the others were transformed. Moreover, as part of his resurrection transformation, Christ's human body took on immortality; he rose never to die again. All of the others who were restored to life in the biblical narratives might have experienced physical restoration and reanimation of their bodies by their souls, but as they were not transformed, they remained corruptible and perishable. They were merely raised back to their old bodies and to the same mortal lives that they had formerly lived, lives that were ultimately headed to the grave once again. And indeed, they did die. We have no record of any of them ascending to heaven as Jesus did, nor are they still with us today. Their experiences are therefore comparable to the healing miracles in the Bible, which did not result in their recipients being unable to get sick or face physical ailments ever again, even as they provided significant temporal relief.

As such, we need to recognise that all of these other raisings were not technically resurrections, but what we might better call 'revivifications', even 'temporary revivifications'. To be sure, the revivifications in the Bible certainly show God's power over death, and they do point forward to the fuller hope of resurrection, but in themselves they are less than Christ's resurrection, which included a transformation to the new life, not a straightforward return to the old.

4

The theological meaning of the gospel

In chapter 1, we made some working assumptions about the relationships between different areas of theology and the gospel. We assumed that those gospels that focused on the event of the cross had atonement as their theological priority, those that focused on the resurrection were more concerned with eschatology, and those that emphasised the lordship of Jesus saw Christ's identity, sovereignty and authority at the heart of the Christian message. At first pass, this all seems reasonable enough, and this is the framework that we will continue to use going forward. However, we must also recognise that there is a good variety of opinions around the scope of these different theologies, perhaps especially atonement theology and eschatology. For example, we saw in chapter 1 that Dodd read all of the events of Jesus' passion, and more, through the lens of eschatology. He thus did not limit the scope of gospel eschatology to only Christ's resurrection, ascension and parousia, but saw it encompassing his death and burial too, those events not being bound up with the separate theological category of atonement. In a similar way, in his *Atonement: A Guide for the Perplexed*, Adam Johnson casts a wide net for the opposite view, saying, 'The atonement is not primarily about overcoming sin – it is first and foremost about giving us life, and life abundantly (Jn 10:10). To put it differently, the atonement is not about death – it is about resurrection.'[1] In this framing, those gospel events elsewhere considered to be eschatological must also be understood through the wide theological lens of atonement. And then McKnight was clear in narrating all of the events of his gospel, which encompassed the whole Bible, into the primary story of the lordship of Christ (see chapter 1 of this volume). Jesus' death and his resurrection are therefore firstly to be understood under the major heading of his rightful sovereignty.

Countless other variations and perspectives from this discussion could be rehearsed, but it is enough to say here that there is no general agreement on the reach of these macro-theological categories, nor on which events of the gospel fit under which heading. Given this, we must accept that different terms can be used differently, and because of this, we need to spell out the ways that we are using the terms in this book, even as we accept that there are other completely valid ways of using them, given that they are synthetic theological categories.

Although some will disagree, 'atonement' probably can lay the greatest claim to being a comprehensive term for everything that Christ achieved in the gospel. At its root, the word simply means 'at-one-ment' and so refers to the process of sinful and estranged human beings being made one with, or coming to have peace with, their holy Creator God. Forgiveness of sins is part of this, as is a personal relationship with the Father, a moral realignment and a hope of spending eternity in union with Christ. Nonetheless, we will here use the word 'atonement' in a more restricted way to refer to the theology of the cross. Some might suggest that 'soteriology' would be a better top-level category here, but there are similar questions around the scope of that term that do not ultimately make it any less ambiguous.

Classically, 'eschatology' is framed around the four last things: death, judgement, heaven and hell, and it is more regularly associated with beliefs about the afterlife of individuals and future of the cosmos, even as some take it more broadly. We will use the word to capture those things, but especially to refer to the theology that flows from Jesus' resurrection, for reasons that will become clear below.

In these two terms, we have two distinct categories for thinking about the theology of the two events of the gospel: Christ's cross ties to atonement and his resurrection to eschatology. Once more, we are not here making any claim that these are the incontestable meanings of each of these terms. Rather, we are simply establishing our usage for the sake of both clarity and utility, as we are particularly concerned to have language that can be used to discuss the theology of the death and resurrection separately and unambiguously, even as it is obviously the case that these interplay with each other at many levels. Beyond the two events of the gospel, we must also consider the sovereignty, authority and lordship of Christ, which naturally sit under the theology that we call Christology, but we will reserve that for the next chapter.

The theology of the cross

As most Christians recognise that the cross of Christ is central to the faith, the literature on its meaning and achievements is vast. In order to make this manageable, various categorisations of the different views have been offered and, although heavily critiqued, it is the taxonomy of Gustav Aulén in his *Christus Victor* that is commonly followed. For simplicity's sake, it is the one that is used here.[2] There are many more understandings of the atonement that do not fit in Aulén's schema, but the three groups of theories that he identifies as being most significant in the history of the church are *Christus Victor* itself, the moral influence theories, and the various satisfaction theories. We will take each of these three in turn, recognising that we can only give the briefest of treatments here.

Christus Victor

Aulén argues that the classic view of the atonement, held since the time of the early church fathers and indeed found in the pages of the New Testament, is that

> Christ – Christus Victor – fights against and triumphs over the evil powers of the world, the 'tyrants' under which mankind [*sic*] is in bondage and suffering, and in Him God reconciles the world to Himself.[3]

What exactly this means has been articulated more recently by N. T. Wright in the following response to a question about how there can be no evil, residual anger or burden of guilt in the new creation:

> First, the death of Jesus himself is seen consistently, albeit multi-facetedly, throughout the New Testament as the means whereby evil is confronted and dealt with. It is defeated, and its power is exhausted, for all that it appears – as the early Christians were only too aware – to have a continuing virulence even after this heavy

> defeat. But second, and based likewise on the death of Jesus, God will forgive; and with that forgiveness God will not only release the world from its burden of guilt but will also, so to speak, release himself from the burden of always having to be angry with a world gone wrong. And, third, in the full outworking of the victory of the cross God will win the final victory over the forces of evil, chaos and death, demonstrating them to be intruders into his good world and overthrowing all the power they have arrogated to themselves.[4]

The promise of God's victory over evil is certainly writ large across the entirety of the Scriptures. It is everywhere from Israel's foundation story of being freed from Egyptian oppressors (Exodus 1–15) through to Jesus' claim to be entering the house of the strong man, Satan, tying him up and plundering his property (Matthew 12:22–29). Paul explains:

> When you were dead in your sins and in the uncircumcision of your flesh, God made you alive with Christ. He forgave us all our sins, having cancelled the charge of our legal indebtedness, which stood against us and condemned us; he has taken it away, nailing it to the cross. And having disarmed the powers and authorities, he made a public spectacle of them, triumphing over them by the cross.
> (Colossians 2:13–15)

It is impossible to deny the prevalence of these themes and the ways that they point to and flow from Christ's death. What is not always immediately clear in this view, however, is exactly *how* Christ's death has achieved the victory over evil. How does the cross confront and deal with evil? How does the crucifixion relate to Jesus binding and plundering Satan? How does Jesus' dying disarm the rulers and authorities? Fleming Rutledge puts it well when she reviews the work of Gerhard Forde on Anselm of Canterbury (whom we will consider below):

> He [Forde] gives Anselm his due, reminding us that Anselm was well aware of the *Christus Victor* theme but found it wanting because *it did not explain why Jesus had to suffer such a brutal death to defeat the demonic forces*. Forde quotes Anselm, asking, 'Why should God

> have to "stoop to such lowly things," or "do anything with such great labor, when he could … just blow the demons away?'"[5]

This is a good question. One answer might be found in the passage of Paul quoted above. In Colossians 2:13–15, it seems that the disarming and shaming of the evil spiritual forces comes as a result of the record of our sins having been nailed to the cross. In Hebrew, the name Satan means 'accuser', consistent with the fact that, in himself, Satan has no authority to condemn anyone of anything, but rather seeks to accuse sinful people before God, whom he knows must bring judgement upon them to be true to his own pure standards of righteousness. But if the punishment for the charges recorded against God's elect have been borne by Christ in his death on the cross, then a just God will not re-punish the same offences again. That would be unjust. In this way, Satan's main power as prosecutor is removed, as there are no longer any offences left to answer for.[6] Evil has been disarmed because it can no longer be placed on the scales of justice in order to bring condemnation on God's people. Or, to put it another way, 'Therefore, there is now no condemnation for those who are in Christ Jesus' (Romans 8:1). The death of Christ takes away one of the only real weapons Satan has: accusations of wrongdoing that attract divine punishment.

Hebrews 2:14–15 adds another dimension to our understanding of the defeat of evil, as it explains that part of the devil's power is holding people in fear of death. But in his resurrection, Christ shows that death has no final victory or 'sting' (1 Corinthians 15:55). To be sure, it is still one of the terrible realities of a fallen world, but it is significantly less frightening for those who have a hope beyond the grave.

It is important to note that in the *Christus Victor* view of the atonement, the problem that Jesus' death resolves is ultimately external to humanity; it is the intrusion of Satan and evil into the world. Humans are therefore victims who need to be rescued from forces beyond themselves even as those forces also penetrate and control them, making them participants in the very evil that seeks to condemn them.

Moral influence

Another way of understanding the achievement of the cross of Christ that has a deep history is as the model for human behaviour *par excellence*. So good is Christ's example that if we follow it without wavering, then we will be walking with God in the path of righteousness. In the twelfth century, the scholastic theologian Peter Abelard wrote that Christ 'has taken our nature on himself, and persevered in this nature, and taught us by both his word and example, even to the point of death', signalling that what Jesus does in his life and his death models what true humanity should be.[7] Abelard goes on to say that the solidarity that Christ has shown by taking on human nature means that 'our hearts should be set on fire' to love Jesus at any cost and without reserve.[8] Jesus has lived as one of us, and now we ought to live like him and for him.

In 1938, Friedrich Schleiermacher, the pioneering and creative German liberal theologian, also championed the idea that Christ's whole life was an example for his people to follow, although he placed particular emphasis on its importance to community building.[9] For Schleiermacher, the work of Christ, which includes his death, models a new way of community living, and no one can really be a follower of Christ unless they are involved in establishing and living out together this new corporate life that captures his enacted priorities. So for both Abelard and Schleiermacher, Christ enables us to be right with God at least in part by showing us a life that God approves of and calling us to live in the same way. Ultimately, this life is lived for the benefit of a particular community, and it will even give itself up to death for that community.

Once more, it would be impossible to suggest that this teaching is not near-central to the Bible's message. Although Philippians 2:6–11 is a passage often cited for its picture of Christ as both humbled and glorified for human salvation, Paul turns to it from verses 3–5 as part of his directive to believers to emulate Jesus even to the point of dying. Christ-copying should be the standard pattern for Christian living. This is also plain from the words of Jesus himself in places like John 15, where he says,

> My command is this: love each other as I have loved you. Greater love has no one than this: to lay down one's life for one's friends. You are my friends if you do what I command.
> (John 15:12–14)

As much as the call to follow Christ in sacrificial living is plain in the New Testament, we must be clear on how dying can be a beneficial part of that. This is really just to ask what Christ's death achieved that was so worthy of imitation. Why could he not have simply set us the example of living a morally outstanding life and then dying peacefully at a ripe old age? How, in short, do the moral influence theories orbit around Christ's death in particular, and not just his outstanding life in general? The answer to these questions is simple enough: in his death, Christ demonstrates that he is prepared to pay the ultimate price for others. He models absolute self-giving for the sake of those he loves, and he calls his people to do the same.

Having said this much, though, we are still no closer to knowing what Christ's death did for us. What did his self-giving give? What did that particular costly sacrifice achieve that benefited others in a way that his continued living would not have done? There is a missing part of the story. On their own, the moral influence theories do not always seem to have obvious answers for this. They have to draw on other theologies of the cross.

Like *Christus Victor*, there is a backwards-looking aspect to the moral influence theories: what Christ has done in the past has lasting impact for his people today. However, the moral influence theories are also very immediately concerned with the active Christian life in the present. They are in some ways a balance to other theories of the atonement that are perceived as being mostly about what people think or where they place their personal trust rather than how their lives are changed and shaped in tangible ways. Unlike *Christus Victor*, the human problem that the moral influence theories foreground is not external evil that results in victimhood, but ignorance that leaves people unclear about how to live in a way that will most please God. But in his life and his death, Christ shows the way. Of course, this is what many casual commentators on the Christian faith understand its main message to be: like all of the world's mainstream religions and philosophies, Christianity essentially offers a guide for good living. Yet, as anyone who looks into Christian beliefs in any depth knows, on its own, this summary does not do justice to fullness of the Bible's teaching.

Satisfaction

The various satisfaction models of the atonement are grounded in the idea that humans owe God some kind of debt, and Christ's death serves to clear that debt on our behalf. Two important versions of the satisfaction model were formulated in the medieval period. In his seminal *Cur Deus Homo*, Anselm of Canterbury argues that humans have not shown God the honour that he deserves, and their lives are unable to pay off the debt for that wrong, but Christ offers his God-honouring life in place of ours.[10] A problem with this formulation is that it does not explain how Christ's death makes up for our dishonouring of God. Certainly, living a life that honours God on our behalf makes sense, but how does dying add to that? The understanding of Thomas Aquinas, the thirteenth-century heavyweight of Roman Catholic theology, perhaps makes more sense. In his *Summa Theologica*, Aquinas sees that the real issue for humanity before God is not one of honour, but one of justice.[11] People have transgressed against God's will, and because God is a God of pure justice, the scales must be balanced; there is a debt of wrongdoing for which a penalty must be paid. Starkly, Romans 6:23 makes plain that 'the wages of sin is death', thus sinful humans ought to die for their offences against God. When we see human guilt foregrounded in this way, it becomes apparent why Christ is needed to substitute not just his holy life for ours, but his death for ours too. In his death, he satisfies God's justice on our behalf.

In the Reformation, the ideas of guilt for sin and Christ's satisfactory substitution were picked up, developed and crystallised to give the meaning of the atonement that is commonplace among many evangelicals today and which goes by the name 'penal substitutionary atonement'.[12] In this formulation, Christ's death is *penal* because God's retributive justice demands a penalty commensurate with any crime or wrongdoing. That this is a priority in God's economy is captured well in the Old Testament's 'eye for eye, tooth for tooth' formula (Leviticus 24:17–22), and it is important to recognise that if God did not respond to our actions so predictably and fairly, he would be morally capricious and open to the charge of being arbitrary in his judgements. As already noted, the just penalty for sin against God is death, and so death is what sinners ought to expect of a just and holy God. This leads straight on to the *substitutionary* dimension of Christ's work on the cross, which is critical to its being for the benefit of others. Substitution is of course a major theme in the Old Testament and is seen most obviously, but by no means exclusively, in Israel's elaborate sacrificial system and rituals for making atonement. The great Day of Atonement documented in Leviticus 16 has the high priest slaughtering a goat as a sin offering and then confessing the sins of the nation over another, which is then cast out into the wilderness, symbolically carrying away the transgressions of the people so they no longer have to carry them themselves. Of course, the goats themselves did not sin, but they bore the sins of the nation. In the same way, Christ himself never sinned, but he bore the death penalty for his people, serving as their substitute. With the death penalty paid by Christ as the substitute for sinners who deserved it, their *atonement* has been accomplished as a free gift of grace. God's people can be one with him, as there is no remaining barrier to their union and fellowship. They are assured of their deliverance from eternal condemnation, as the price for their sins has been fully paid by Christ.

Within penal substitutionary atonement, the fact that Christ died in place of his people and carried off humanity's sin is at the core of the grace of the gospel, 'grace' being defined by Martin Luther's trusted co-worker Philip Melanchthon as God's favour shown to people who do not deserve it.[13] It is easy to see why the grace-soaked gospel of penal substitutionary atonement is rightly celebrated as good news. Indeed, it is hard to imagine better news.

Where the *Christus Victor* model of the atonement addresses the problem of external evil and the moral influence theories address human ignorance and motivation, the satisfaction models of atonement address the guilt and culpability that results from hearts that are turned away from God and the actions that go against his will. All of the problems that the different models address can be traced right back to the garden of Eden, although it is perhaps guilt that is most on view there (Genesis 3).

There are many, many objections to this penal substitutionary understanding of the atonement, including the question of whether God really requires penalties to be paid for wrongdoings, the conviction that God cannot have wrath at sin as that would be contradictory to his loving nature, the belief that only a selective reading of the Bible can arrive at such a narrow view and more besides. As much as these critiques do require responses – and many responses have been made – they do not finally undercut penal substitution when it is charitably and biblically understood, and they often do not offer alternate models of the atonement that are less problematic.[14] One clarification that is important to make any time that penal substitution is discussed is that when Christ was crucified, God the Father was not punishing the Son. Rather, the Father and the Son and the Spirit were all working in harmonious union to punish sin, with the Son willingly giving himself up to bear this punishment for the sake of his people. There is complete unity and shared, deep love within the Trinity in the work of atonement.

In terms of giving a theology of the cross that explains why Christ died, and that gels with much of the rest of the teaching of the New Testament, penal substitutionary atonement has excellent explanatory power.

Other models

As noted at the start of the chapter, there are countless more theories of the atonement beyond those sketched above, many of which also have a number of different expressions. For example, there is the ransom theory, which sees Christ given to Satan as a payment to redeem humanity; the fish-hook theory (which is noted by Aulén), in which Satan takes the 'bait' of Christ's humanity in death but is then caught and destroyed by the invisible 'hook' of his divinity; recapitulation, in which Christ replays the history of either Adam or Israel without falling into sin; and the governmental theory, in which Christ is representatively punished in place of sinners without a one-for-one accounting of each sin and transgression. All of these theories have their merits, and each contributes something to our understanding of what Christ's death achieved. Again, space does not permit the full exploration of them that a volume dedicated to atonement would.

But there is one other view that is worth expanding a little, as it ties directly back to Christ's death by means of public crucifixion. This view is helpfully outlined in the writings of Moltmann and could be called 'absolute solidarity'. Moltmann writes,

> But in taking his way to the cross, Jesus was also making his own decision: his active love for sufferers becomes his suffering love with sufferers. We understand his suffering obedience to God not as his sacrifice for the sins of the world but as his unreserved self-giving to the uttermost for the God-forsaken … The Godness of God manifested in Jesus' surrender of himself to death on the cross is a love which is capable not only of suffering but even of the fate of death. So from this 'love of God which is in Christ Jesus' (Rom 8.39) even 'tribulation, distress, persecution, famine or sword' can no longer separate us (8.35) …
>
> If God goes where Jesus goes, if God himself was in Jesus, then through his passion Jesus brings the love of God to people who are as cast down and emptied as he was himself …
>
> His cross is a brother's cross that stands among the crosses of this world, as a sign – yes, as a revelation – that God himself participates in our pain, and that he is beside us in our forsakenness.[15]

In this view, Jesus' death demonstrates his unwavering solidarity with those suffering in a sin-filled world. Although he was the all-powerful Son of God, he chose not to use that power to escape the pain and injustice of his execution. He could have done exactly what those witnessing his death had called him to do and freed himself from the cross in a show of divine power, but instead he stayed on it as a display of divine love (Matthew 27:39–44). What Jesus shows in refusing to abandon the cross is that God *always* takes the side of the broken and struggling, no matter what the cost. When the 'Godforsaken' and those 'cast down' look to the cross, they learn that God does not retreat from the struggles of life to the security of his greater power, nor does he draw on strengths they do not have to ensure a better outcome for himself. Instead, he remains absolutely one with them in their circumstances, even to the point of death. From this, they draw strength in knowing that no matter what they suffer or what they must face, God is on their side. They need never fear that God forgets them or distances himself from their situation, even if that means that he must stay with them to the most bitter end.

One unified event, many cascading benefits

It is not hard to see that many of the different views of the atonement have some validity as they each cast a different light on the multidimensional meaning of Christ's death. No single view, therefore, should be absolutely championed at the complete expense of all of the others. What can be asked, however, is whether the different views relate to one another in meaningful ways. Is an integration of the different aspects of atonement theology possible, or can they only be considered as separate entries on a list of options?

We have already seen some of the connections between the different perspectives, and we can quickly reiterate some of them here, choosing to use the penal substitutionary view as the starting point, and then noting some of the ways that it is centrally bound up with the others.[16] What we are not able to work towards here is any sort of final or comprehensive list of theological links between the various theories of the atonement; that would be a phenomenal exercise. Rather, all we want to do is flag a few simple examples to underscore that some such connections do exist, and it would therefore be unhelpfully restrictive to think about the atonement in either just one way, or as having a collection of unrelated aspects. So, we noted that penal substitution makes sense of the death of Christ as a sacrifice provided in order to meet the justice and wrath of God against human sin. But it is in offering himself completely like this that Christ also gives the moral example by which his people should live as he demonstrates the importance of putting the greatest needs of others before any needs of our own. If the problem of human sin is paramount, then Christ offers an extraordinary example of living for the benefit of others by dying in order to meet their greatest need and deal with that problem. Furthermore, in his death, which pays the price for sin, humans are ransomed, and God has his victory over Satan, whose powers of accusation are rendered impotent. Similarly, the evil of the human heart is subdued, as God releases people from the need to take vengeance or seek rough justice because they see that Christ deals not only with their sins, but also the sins that others have committed against them. His death meets all of the requirements of justice, allowing his people to embrace the freedom of not needing to make things right themselves and of not being trapped in bitterness. Finally, in his death, Christ shows his complete solidarity with those who suffer as he takes away the sins of the world, which lead to all of the suffering in the first place. However, he not only shares in their problems but also fixes them.

To be sure, this is a too-quick and simplistically neat way of tying together the different theories of atonement, and it would not be hard to find loose ends or some misfitting pieces in such a clipped synthesis. But nonetheless, it ought to be enough to demonstrate that, far from being alternatives vying for the title of *the* interpretation of the event of Jesus' death, the major theological understandings of the atonement overlap and interrelate to give us a fuller picture of the meaning and purpose of the cross. Through Christ's death comes our forgiveness, our moral example, the defeat of the powers of evil and the assurance of his commitment to us. Penal substitutionary atonement might be the centrepiece, but it is also the linchpin that holds together many different dimensions of what Jesus' crucifixion means.

The theology of the resurrection

In recent generations, some quarters of the evangelical world have tended to give more attention to the meaning of Christ's death, or at least certain aspects of its meaning, than to understanding the event of his death from which that meaning flows. At the same time, there conversely appears to have been far more clarity regarding some of the material and historical facts of Christ's resurrection than there has been on its theological meaning and purpose. Indeed, it often seems that Jesus' words, 'It is finished' (John 19:30), spoken from the cross, have been taken to indicate not only that his suffering was over, but also that at that moment, he had completed absolutely everything that he came to do. In this way of thinking, Christ's resurrection becomes something of an epilogue, a happy ending to a sad story or some sort of validation that the work of atonement had truly been accomplished by his death. Consider the following from E. W. Bullinger on the idea that the resurrection is essentially the confirmation of the effectiveness of the cross:

> Christ's death justified His People. When, therefore, He was raised again from the dead, that resurrection was the declaration of it – the

> Divine promulgation of the decree pronouncing our justification. His resurrection is our receipt, the evidence to us that our debt has been paid and the bond cancelled. His blood was not the receipt, but *the price*. His death was not the receipt, but it was *the payment* of the debt. His resurrection, therefore, is *the receipt for that payment*.[17]

Here, the resurrection does not achieve anything in and of itself; it is simply the proof and proclamation that Christ's death has succeeded in making atonement for his people. If there had been no resurrection, all that would have been lost is a piece of evidence for what the cross had accomplished. Not only is this a thin understanding of the resurrection, it is also not immediately clear how Christ's resurrection serves as this 'receipt'. How does the resurrection show that Christ's death achieved justification, paid our debt and cancelled our bond? If it does show those things, Bullinger has not offered the explanatory link here.

For a helpful response to the resurrection-as-receipt idea, we can turn to Richard Gaffin, who writes,

> The resurrection is nothing if not his [Christ's] deliverance from the power and curse of death which was in force until the moment of being raised … it and no other event in his experience is the point of his transition from wrath to grace. This does not at all imply that Paul compromises the absolute necessity and intrinsic efficacy of Christ's death (as an atonement). It does mean, however, that he does not confuse the ransom price, no matter how sublime and precious, with what is secured by its payment.[18]

Now Christ's resurrection is not the receipt for the payment of the debt, but it is 'what is secured by its payment'. That is, the resurrection is not just proof that the cross worked, it is what the work of the cross enabled and opened up. For Gaffin, Christ's resurrection can be understood to some degree as the goal, while his cross is the means by which the goal is achieved, and this seems to accord more with the biblical picture. Recognising that resurrection is the gateway to eternal life for all who follow Jesus, we can note that this is where the most famous verse in John's Gospel leads:

> For God so loved the world that he gave his one and only Son, that whoever believes in him shall not perish but have eternal life. (John 3:16)

God gave his only Son over to death, in order that those who believe shall have eternal life, that is, resurrection life. The cross is the means and resurrection is the end. If the justification of the cross were the end in itself, and the resurrection was just the 'receipt', then the verse might instead read:

> For God so loved the world that he gave his one and only Son, that whoever believes in him shall not be unrighteous but shall be justified, and the resurrection confirms this.

This might indeed be true, and we certainly want to join with Gaffin in affirming what we have said earlier in this chapter: for Paul and the New Testament as a whole, Christ's death is absolutely necessary and intrinsically effective for making atonement. But this is not the primary thing that John 3:16 is communicating. Instead, it accords with the idea that to stand in the presence of God for all eternity, a person must first have the debt and stain of their sin removed and their hearts reoriented towards him, for God cannot abide guilt and rebellion in his presence, and these equally have no place in his new creation. Therefore, an atonement is required to bring forgiveness and cleansing to God's people and to make each one, and all of them collectively, a fitting dwelling place for the Holy Spirit, who brings and sustains the new and eternal life into which they can now enter. The Spirit-filled eternal resurrection life is not just an endless continuation of the same life as lived before death, but entails much more, which our fuller theology of the resurrection spells out for us.

The simplest way to explore the richness of resurrection theology is to consider a number of its aspects separately, even as we acknowledge the final falseness of making such separations. Ultimately, resurrection theology must be recognised as a multidimensional but closely integrated whole, as is the case for the atonement theology of the cross. Nonetheless, considering different dimensions of the resurrection apart from one another helps us to see each more clearly.

First, we must acknowledge that it is true that the resurrection witnesses to the effectiveness of the cross. Simplistically, we could say that it does this by demonstrating that Jesus' words were true. He repeatedly predicted his own death and resurrection, and because both happened, we can believe all of his words, including those about his death. Of course, Jesus did not explain at length in his predictions what his death would accomplish, and so the resurrection does not clearly prove our atonement theology, but only Jesus' trustworthiness more generally. More helpfully, in 1 Corinthians 15:17, Paul writes, 'if Christ has not been raised, your faith is futile; you are still in your sins.' Here, Paul argues that if the resurrection of Christ did not occur, then it would be clear that the cross had not been that means of forgiveness and cleansing that allowed for God's people to stand eternally in his presence.

Second, and most obviously, Jesus' resurrection shows that there is new life after death. Death is not the end, nor does it permanently lock people away in a shadowy underworld or some disembodied state (even if there is a lot to unpack here about the intermediate state between death and resurrection). As obvious as this is, we must not fail to notice its significance. Along with the question of the purpose of life, the question of what happens after we die is one of the greatest existential questions that presses upon all people in every age and every culture. The major world religions all have strong answers to this, as too do nihilism and even materialistic atheism. The difference, however, is that in the Christian faith, beliefs around the afterlife are supported by the historical fact of Christ's resurrection. Christians do not speculate on what they imagine *might* happen after death, they simply report what *did* happen to Jesus. They do not try to develop reasonable-sounding theories or comforting ideas; they simply point to an event. To the question of what happens after death, Christians can respond confidently that there is a new life because our forebears witnessed it. To be sure, other faiths might make proof claims for their view of the afterlife, but none are quite the same as this.

Third, in Christ's resurrection, his followers see not only that there is life after death, but also what that life is like. Paul's teaching in 1 Corinthians 15 is not only about Jesus in his resurrection, but also about resurrection generally. In fact, in that chapter, Paul is not making the case for Christ's resurrection, as that was a widely accepted fact in the early church. Rather, he was teaching about the general resurrection that all humanity will experience at Christ's return, and he uses Christ's resurrection as the grounds for his case. Just as we know what it was for Christ, so too it will be for all of us. We have some idea of what our eternal nature will be like because we have witnesses to Christ in his eternal nature. Paul uses the powerful language of firstfruits to expand this teaching, and we will consider that more closely in the next chapter.

Fourth and following on, in Christ's resurrection, humanity is made fit to enter the presence of God. Mortal and fallen flesh can neither inherit nor inhabit the final state of the kingdom, where God will be known and seen face to face (1 Corinthians 13:12; Revelation 22:4). Only transformed, resurrected people can be brought into the direct presence of the Father. This is a fascinating idea to pursue, as it suggests that even Adam and Eve in their unfallen state could not have had the fullness of a completely constant and unimpeded relationship with God – an understanding that dates back at least as far as Bishop Irenaeus of Lyon in the second century.[19] Sin was not in their way, and yet the homes of God and mortals were separate, with God inhabiting the highest heavens above and humanity occupying the created world below, even if God would sometimes visit the garden (Genesis 3:8). It will only be in the future, as foreseen at the end of the book of Revelation, that the dwelling place of God will be among mortals (Revelation 21:3). This is not a 'return to the garden of Eden', but rather the settlement of the new creation's 'garden city', which has been the goal of creation since the beginning and which is only fit for those cleansed by the atonement and made new in the resurrection.[20] New creation people belong in the new creation, and old creation people do not.

Fifth and complementarily, in Christ's resurrection, creation is endorsed. Rather than leaving his old body to rot away and his soul to live on independently, rather than having his old body sloughed off and replaced by an entirely new body, God raised Christ's same body from the dead, but he healed it and transformed it to its new creation state. This shows that God's plan is not to abandon or reject the creation he made in favour of another, but to remake it and renew it. It is good for us to remember that God loves our bodies as integral to who we are. Indeed, he made us 'very good' as enfleshed beings (Genesis 1:31). Similarly, the whole creation was made good in God's eyes, and it is not his ultimate plan to be rid of it, but instead, to have it come to the fullness of what it was always going to be. While we know that the transformation of our bodies will be after the pattern of Christ's resurrection body, the Bible does not offer a clear picture of what the transformation of the rest of creation will be like. Some places in the New Testament, such as 2 Peter 3:10, speak of the time when 'The heavens will disappear with a roar; the elements will be destroyed by fire', but this is best read not as a prediction of the destruction of creation before the establishment of an entirely new creation, but rather as evocative language highlighting how fully the current creation will be purged of sin and evil, even more than it was during the Genesis flood. If we also understand Christ as not just the firstborn from among the dead, but also the first part of the new creation (Colossians 1:18),[21] then we can fairly suggest that the world will be transformed in some manner akin to the transformation of human resurrection. God's plan is to renew the whole creation, and he has begun that work in Christ. If this point is correct, then we can go beyond saying that resurrection is part of Christian eschatology, or that eschatology is best seen through the lens of Christ's resurrection, to make the statement that resurrection is eschatology. That is, what the Bible presents of the cosmic future – restoration, transformation, continuity, eternity, glory – is nothing more than the spreading outwards of what we see of Christ in his resurrection. Resurrection is the essence of all that God has prepared for his entire creation.

Sixth and following on briefly, if Christ's resurrection marks the beginning of the general resurrection of all people, which in turn is part of the renewal of the whole creation, we can say that the age of the new creation has dawned. While in the Genesis 1 account of the first creation, humankind was made on the last day of God's work, things are inverted in the new creation, with the new humanity first realised in Christ as its beginning. Christ thus stands at the centre of the whole story of creation to new creation, being the 'last Adam', the pinnacle person of the pinnacle species in the first creation and the pioneer and head of the new creation after which and from which all else will follow. Therefore, we can think of Christ's resurrection as 'day one' of the new creation, which is yet to be completed, but which has already begun.[22]

Seventh, the resurrection of Christ guarantees that justice will be served on earth. This might not be as intuitive as some of the other points, but it makes sense when we recognise that Christ is to be the judge of the world. When calling the Athenians to repent in Acts 17:30–31, Paul warns them that the future judgement is certain because the appointed judge has been raised from the dead. The logic is that if Christ had remained dead, then there would be no eternal judge that all would have to face, but as he has been raised to ongoing life, there is, and he will pass judgement on the last day.

Eighth and finally, the resurrection of Christ shapes not only our future hope, but also how we live right now. It is perhaps under-realised that all of Christian ethics can be well-understood as an expression of resurrection living.[23] Ephesians 2:5 speaks of Christians being made alive with Christ, and verse 6 says that we have been raised up and 'seated … with him in the heavenly realms'. Paul's language makes it sound as though Jesus' followers have already been resurrected and even translated to heaven before their deaths. But while this is not the case materially, Paul wants us to see it as our true identity. He wants us to understand ourselves as resurrection people and so to live out resurrection lives. Colossians 3 expands the idea. In that chapter, Paul calls Christians to put to death behaviours and attitudes that do not align with God's will and instead to clothe themselves with those that do, essentially to be morally transformed from godless people to godly people. But no one is called to do this from a bare sense of duty, nor by sheer willpower, nor out of fear of the consequences of non-compliance. Paul opens the chapter by indicating that Christians are people who have been 'raised with Christ' and who therefore should 'set [their] hearts on things above, where Christ is, seated at the right hand of God' (Colossians 3:1). He is saying that Christians are to live their risen lives now, to be actively who they have become as members of Christ's body. We can perhaps expand this and say that Paul is not calling Christians only to act as though they are already living the fully spiritual Christian life that characterises resurrected people, but also to recognise that just as the resurrection of humanity has begun in Jesus, so too our own resurrections have begun at the moral level, even if not yet the physical. Indeed, it is precisely because believers have already begun to be raised in this way that they live Christlike lives. We refrain from stealing not only because it is forbidden and we are frightened of the punishment, but because resurrection people do not steal. We do not commit adultery just because we have calculated that it never turns out well or because our community would shun us if we did, but because transformed people do not commit adultery. We do not murder simply because we could not get away with it, or even because we feel that it would disrespect God who has given life to all, but because the risen life is not a murderous life. To be sure, obeying God's will, living thankfully, valuing our place in the church, respecting God's creation and avoiding repercussions are all healthy enough motivations for good behaviour. But understanding ourselves as resurrection people goes deeper still, right to the core of our identity. And there should not be the slightest bit of tedium or frustration in it either, no sense that only dry duty leads us to live for Jesus. Rather, we celebrate and rejoice in the gloriousness of being resurrection people like and along with our Lord.

Far from being only an apologetic for the cross, the resurrection is full of hugely important meaning. Resurrection theology in no way diminishes the importance of the atonement, but neither can it all be assumed under the work of the cross or made completely derivative of atonement. Good Friday and Easter Day mark different events in the life of Christ, and while the meanings of those events are expressed in ways that are certainly related, they are significantly distinct too.

*

It should be plain that our brief consideration of the theologies of the cross and resurrection has only just scratched the surface. Already, we can see how much further these truths could spill over and flow into the many different spheres of Christian life and belief. And recognising this actually aligns with one of the major contentions of this book: that the gospel is the hub of all Christian theology. We will pick up and expand on this more in chapter 7, but next we must turn to the question of why the gospel really only works if Jesus is the God-man that orthodox theology has presented him to be for over 1,500 years.

5

Why the gospel needs the God-man

The identity of the incarnate Jesus as both fully human and fully divine lies at the conceptual heart of orthodox Christology, and it is also where most Christological studies place their emphasis. This is good and necessary, as over the course of Western theological history, many of the errors in understanding who Jesus is have grown from defending one of his two natures to the detriment of the other. Either his true humanity is secured by diminishing his divinity or his true divinity is secured by diminishing his humanity.[1] Neither position reflects the biblical witness. Another mistake that has been made is taking Jesus as part true God and part true man. This is an attempt to preserve something of his two natures, but it actually ends up diluting them both. Given that the New Testament writers are very eager for us not to compromise either the humanity or the deity of Jesus in any way, and given the theological dangers of doing so, we are thankful that the church's thinkers maintain their commitment to presenting and defending these twinned truths.

In this book, however, our purpose is not to go over these theological foundations of Jesus' incarnation, but to take them as given and to turn our attention to a consideration of the necessity of his being fully God and fully human to the workings of the gospel. At a technical level, we want to look at the junction of the doctrines of the incarnation and the gospel and, less technically, we want to show why the gospel simply does not work if Christ did not exist in his two natures. If the two gospel events are that Christ died for our sins and that he has been raised on the third day, the question now is why it had to be Christ, the incarnate God-man. Why could it not have been someone else or something else (for example, a sacrificial animal) that died and rose? Why could it not have been Jesus as a human only? Or as God only? As we walk through this matter systematically, we will find that the identity of the dual-natured Messiah is absolutely essential not only to the faithful proclamation of the gospel, but also (if we can momentarily speak this way) to the effective *functioning* of the gospel. It is because the person and identity of Christ are so central and important to the gospel that Christology really needs to sit alongside his death and resurrection as the third pillar of gospel theology alongside atonement and eschatology.

Who is this man?

The Gospels of Matthew, Mark and Luke all reach key turning points when Peter declares the identity of Jesus. Despite some of the Christological controversies of the early church, it was not challenging for those who met Jesus in the flesh to accept that he was a real human being. He looked and lived just like any other human, and his earthly family and life story were well known (for example, Matthew 13:54–56). However, once he began his public ministry, it became clear that he was a person of significant note; his miracles, healings and teaching made this undeniable. After a time, Jesus took up the issue of his identity directly with his disciples. Matthew's version of the encounter reads,

> When Jesus came to the region of Caesarea Philippi, he asked his disciples, 'Who do people say the Son of Man is?'
>
> They replied, 'Some say John the Baptist; others say Elijah; and still others, Jeremiah or one of the prophets.'
>
> 'But what about you?' he asked. 'Who do you say I am?'
>
> Simon Peter answered, 'You are the Messiah, the Son of the living God.'
>
> Jesus replied, 'Blessed are you, Simon son of Jonah, for this was not revealed to you by flesh and blood, but by my Father in heaven.' (Matthew 16:13–17)

It is clear from this conversation that there was a general consensus that Jesus was at least comparable to the famous prophets of God. But at the same time, most people were not suggesting that he was more than a human prophet through whom God was working just as he had worked through John the Baptist, Elijah, Jeremiah and others. However, Peter's own assessment makes the great leap. He declares that Jesus is 'the Messiah, the Son of the Living God'. By recognising Jesus as Messiah, Peter is first of all maintaining his understanding that Jesus is a human being. To be sure, the Messiah was the divinely appointed ruler of God's people like the great kings of the Old Testament including David and Solomon – and indeed the great messiah that Israel was expecting was to be of the royal line of David – but still the title was a human one. However, Peter then couples this affirmation with the belief that Jesus is the very Son of the living God, that is, a divine being sharing a common nature with the Father.

Although, to modern ears, the title 'Son of God' sounds straightforwardly like what Peter ultimately means here, in first-century Palestine, it was a little more complex. Roman emperors were often presented and received as sons of the gods, and even the Old Testament has a range of references to sons of God that are not all transparently about the Second Person of the Trinity, but could at least initially refer to human (or other) beings.[2] Nonetheless, one of the conclusions that the New Testament wants its readers to reach is that Jesus really is the Son of God in a unique way, a way that places him as equal to God the Father and finally insists that he is not only the Son of God but even God the Son. In his response to Jesus' question, Peter seems to be openly declaring this truth. Of course, this is a radical statement to make, and Jesus commends it, even saying that Peter's knowledge has come from God himself. Jesus is indeed rightly recognised as the God-man. He is both the royal Son of David and the divine Son of God.

Interestingly, what comes next strongly connects the identity of Jesus to the gospel message. From this point on in their narratives, all of the first three written Gospels switch their focus. Previously, their overarching question had been about who this man is. Now, it shifts to what he was here to do. If this God-man has turned up in world history, what is his purpose in doing that? Completely in line with the definition of the gospel that we found in 1 Corinthians, the answer in each of the Synoptic Gospels soon comes, three times repeated, from Jesus' own lips: the God-man came to die and rise again.[3] Similarly, in John 5:17–18, there is a critical turning point. It comes not when Peter recognises that

Jesus is divine as well as human, but when the Jews in Jerusalem realise that he is making that claim for himself. After this, he becomes their sworn enemy such that 'they tried all the more to kill him', an intention that would eventually lead to his crucifixion and resurrection. Both the stories of the Gospels and the distilled gospel message hinge on these two events, but they also depend on the recognition that they were the actions of the divine-human Messiah. 1 Corinthians 15 says, '*Christ* died for our sins … and *he* has been raised again on the third day' (my translation). It does not say that a lamb or a bull or a goat died and was raised again, the first part of which might not have turned so many heads in the ancient Jewish world. It says that *Christ* died and rose, with the title 'Christ' here carrying a lot of freight.

Why a human needed to die

At least since Anselm of Canterbury in the eleventh century, it has been well understood that God needed to take on flesh precisely so he was able to die. Without becoming incarnate, there could have been no ripping apart of his body and soul, both of which are properties of his humanity.[4] The Creator God cannot die, but created humans can and do, and so if Jesus had to truly die, he had to be truly human. This is basic to our understanding of why the gospel needs Jesus to be human, but it is not the only reason.

In Jesus and Peter's conversation discussed above, it is clear that Jesus cannot be known rightly without pushing past the possibility that he is a prophet like those of the Old Testament. A similar interaction unfolds quite differently in the opening chapter of John's Gospel. Here, the Jewish leaders interrogate John the Baptist as to his identity. Not only does he refuse to associate himself with Israel's prophets – although Jesus would later contradict him on this – but he is also completely clear that he is *not* the Messiah (John 1:19–28, cf. Matthew 11:14). The very next scene that the Fourth Gospel records is John pointing out Jesus, but interestingly he does not do that by calling him the Messiah, but by saying, 'Look, the Lamb of God, who takes away the sin of the world!' (John 1:29). Although familiar to lots of Christians today, this statement is strange. Why did John use those words?

What would not have been strange to the people within earshot of John was the idea that a lamb could take away sin. Indeed, since the days of Moses, the religious life of Israel revolved around an elaborate system of animal sacrifices and offerings that the priests would make on behalf of the people. Among the several reasons for making such offerings was atonement – restoring unity with God after sinning – and one of the animals that it was permissible to bring for a sin offering was a lamb. Leviticus 4 outlines the process:

> If someone brings a lamb as their sin offering, they are to bring a female without defect. They are to lay their hand on its head and slaughter it for a sin offering at the place where the burnt offering is slaughtered. Then the priest shall take some of the blood of the sin offering with his finger and put it on the horns of the altar of burnt offering and pour out the rest of the blood at the base of the altar. They shall remove all the fat, just as the fat is removed from the lamb of the fellowship offering, and the priest shall burn it on the altar on top of the food offerings presented to the LORD. In this way the priest will make atonement for them for the sin they have committed, and they will be forgiven.
> (Leviticus 4:32–35)

This is a precise, costly and bloody exercise. A female lamb without defect would have been prized not only in itself, but also because of its great potential to rear more high-quality stock in the future. To offer it up in a ritual would have been a measurable material sacrifice to its owners. But the expense would have been thought worthwhile to secure forgiveness and the re-establishment of a right relationship with God.

Following what we saw in the last chapter, this is a version of penal substitutionary atonement. The penalty for sin is death. A lamb is substituted for the sinner who identifies with it by placing their hand on its head. The result is being at one with God as the debt for sin is counted to be discharged, satisfying God's justice. Such sacrifices were important and frequent in Israel's history, something that is brought into sharp relief when it is remembered that the great temple, which was the heart of Jewish religion and around which the city and life of Jerusalem was built (and the tabernacle that preceded it during the decades from the exodus through to the rule of King Solomon), was on one level a great slaughterhouse. Its courts were designed for the presentation and killing of substitutionary animals by the thousands, and all of God's people were expected to participate in these sacrifices throughout their lives. Thus, had John the Baptist pointed to someone leading a sheep to the temple and said, 'Look, a lamb that takes away sin,' few people would have found it particularly remarkable. He would have been drawing attention to something that, while serious, was quite commonplace. Animals died for sins all of the time, and the people of God were used to certain animals taking their place in death. But John pointed to Jesus, identifying him as the 'Lamb of God'. It was strange.

What John recognised, and what he was calling others to recognise, was that the entire Old Testament sacrificial system was coming to its completion in Jesus. While certain bleeding animals could stand in for human beings under that system, the final reality was that they were not of the same nature as humans and were therefore not truly fitting substitutes. The sacrificial system did not work with an 'eye for eye, tooth for tooth' equivalence in either physical or moral terms; a strict *lex talionis* ('law of exact retaliation') did not apply (cf. Leviticus 24:17–22). And while the grace of God allowed for this substitution of lesser for greater under the old covenant, the pure justice of God could never finally be met this way. As the book of Hebrews makes explicit, ultimately, 'it is impossible for the blood of bulls and goats to take away sins' (Hebrews 10:4); they were merely placeholders that foreshadowed the costly sacrifice that was really needed, and they provided an object for the people's faith in the grace of God until that final sacrifice was made. So even as the Old Testament sacrificial system was an effective proxy for a time, in the end, a human being was needed to bear the punishment for human guilt if there was to be true justice and a valid, equivalent substitution for those who had sinned. To make final atonement, Jesus had to be truly human.

Why God needed to die

We saw in the last chapter that Christ's death was required to pay the price for sin, to take away Satan's accusatory power, to set the ultimate example of living for others and to show complete solidarity with those suffering in the world. Now we ask why all of these things could not have been achieved by just an outstanding, even perfect, human being. Why does the gospel need God himself to die? Calvin offers one answer:

> Robbers and other malefactors contumaciously hasten to death, many men [*sic*] magnanimously despise it, others meet it calmly. If the Son of God was amazed and terror-struck at the prospect of it, where was his firmness or magnanimity? We are even told, what in a common death would have been deemed most extraordinary, that in the depth of his agony his sweat was like great drops of blood falling to the ground. Nor was this a spectacle exhibited to the eyes of others, since it was from a secluded spot that he uttered his groans to his Father. And that no doubt may remain, it was necessary that angels should come down from heaven to strengthen him with miraculous consolation. How shamefully effeminate would it have been (as I have observed) to be so excruciated by the fear of an ordinary death as to sweat great drops of blood, and not even be revived by the presence of angels? What? Does not that prayer, thrice repeated, 'Father, if it be possible, let this cup pass from me' (Matth. xxvi. 39), a prayer dictated by incredible bitterness of soul, show that Christ had a fiercer and more arduous struggle than with ordinary death?[5]

Rejecting Calvin's outdated characterisation of femininity as we go, we see that his main point here is that Christ's death must have been *unlike* normal human death, which many are able to face with dignity and calm hearts and without sweating blood or receiving angelic support (notwithstanding that these experiences of Christ are unlikely to be part of the original text of Luke's Gospel from which Calvin drew them).[6] According to Calvin, Christ's was a 'fiercer and more arduous struggle' than others go through when facing their end. Jesus had some kind of intensified experience of death; he faced a different kind of death than other people face. If this is correct, we could argue that it had to be God the incarnate Son who died because no regular, non-divine human could have endured the intensity of the unique kind of death that was needed in order to make atonement. An extraordinary death required someone more than human.

Although there is a logic to this view, it is not without serious problems. One is that it downplays the severity of all human death. Calvin is assuming that those who took to death more easily than Jesus did were making a correct assessment of it; they were right not to feel overly distraught at normal human death. While this is possible, it is also reasonable to suggest that those people had failed to grapple with the true horror of death, as do so many today. They take death relatively lightly because they have not actually stared deeply into the abyss. Jesus was not like this. When facing the reality of the death of his friend Lazarus, for example, he wept, and that was even knowing that he was about to reverse it (John 11:32–36). Jesus felt how raw and horrific and anti-creation death is. Indeed, when it is pondered in all of its starkness, death is something that most human psychologies cannot automatically face with peace, and it seems fair to conclude that Christ's terror in facing his own death was not because it was a different kind of death, but simply because he was prepared to look at death directly and honestly, and he saw its terrifying reality with great clarity.

The second issue with Calvin's view follows on: he suggests that there are different kinds of death. Is there a 'normal' death, which we might call 'biological' and which all living things face, but then also a different death that is more intense, perhaps involving spiritual suffering as it includes the judgemental wrath of God? Assuming for a moment that this is the case, we need to ask if this is what Jesus faced on the cross in place of normal death, or if it is the death that comes after the 'normal', first death as seems to be indicated by texts such as Luke 12:4–5 and Revelation 20:13–15, although we do not know that Christ died any second death after his 'normal' death. Perhaps there is a third type of death, one that all deserve to suffer but which only Christ ever endured on behalf of the elect but not the reprobate. At this point, matters are becoming quite speculative and complicated, and even if there is something that is right somewhere in this line of thinking, we can also find more straightforward reasons that the gospel needed the death of Christ as God.

One of these harks back to Leviticus requiring a lamb without blemish as the sacrificial offering. This was captured in the satisfaction views put forward by both Anselm and Aquinas, which demonstrated that in order to be worthy, the atoning sacrifice had to be pure, without any history of dishonouring God or offending against his will.[7] If it was not, then it would not be offering anything better than sinful humanity could offer, and an impure offering does not make up for impure lives. The late Tim Keller and his wife Kathy put it well in the twenty-third question and answer of the *New City Catechism*:

> Q: Why must the Redeemer be truly God?
> A: That because of his divine nature his obedience and suffering would be perfect and effective.[8]

No non-divine human could ever satisfy the honour and justice of God because no such human can be so pure as to offer a perfect, and therefore a worthy, sacrifice in God's eyes. The fact that sin has deceived, entrapped, misguided and stained all of humanity is the reason that the substitute needed to be a divine being, who was uniquely able to resist sin and avoid all of its impacts on his purity and who was therefore uniquely worthy to meet God's requirement for justice.

Third, if it were not God who died for the sins of the world, then his grace towards humanity shown in the gospel would have been significantly different and potentially significantly less than we know it to be. That is because, in Christ, God himself bears away the consequences for sin. This means that if Christ were not God, then humanity's sins would only have been punished in humanity; humanity alone would bear the sins of humanity. In that scenario, God might have been gracious in providing an acceptable human sacrifice, were it possible to find one among fallen humanity, and that would certainly have been a blessing to those other humans whose sins were borne away. But it would not mark the removal of the punishment for sin from creaturely humanity as a whole. John the Baptist said that the Lamb of God takes away the sin of the world, not that he only transfers it from some of the world's creatures to another. God's grace is that *he* makes the sacrifice, which is sufficient to take sin away from every member of the human race and indeed from the whole of creation. Furthermore, if it was the case that a regular human could take away human sin, then humanity would not finally need God. The human race would not be totally depraved after all, and it could make a way to heaven on its own, without the grace of God, just as the builders of the tower of Babel believed that they could (Genesis 11:1–4). But given that this is not possible, God had to be in Christ reconciling the world to himself (2 Corinthians 5:19).

Why a human needed to rise

In the previous chapter, we considered some of the theological significances of the resurrection. For a number of these to be directly applicable to humanity, it was essential that Christ himself was a true human being. For example, if Christ was not fully human, then humans would have no direct model for their own resurrected future and nothing concrete to look to for our future hope. We could confirm that resurrection was a possibility for a divine being, but no more. If Christ was not human, then it would not be clear that humanity will be made fit to enter into the presence of God, as there would be no precedent for that. We could say that divine figures may access one another's direct presence, but who could say if humans could too? And if Christ was not fully human, then his resurrection would not be an endorsement of God's creation because nothing properly belonging to that first creation would have been confirmed as continuing through to the new creation. We would have no confidence that God so approved of the stuff of this world that his plan is to renew and restore it rather than just replace it or even abandon it altogether.

At the root of all of these observations is Paul's idea in 1 Corinthians 15:20 that Christ is 'the firstfruits of those who have fallen asleep [died]', with the 'firstfruits' language being drawn from Leviticus 23, a text rich with allusions to the gospel:

> The Lord said to Moses, 'Speak to the Israelites and say to them: "When you enter the land I am going to give you and you reap its

> harvest, bring to the priest a sheaf of the first grain you harvest. He is to wave the sheaf before the LORD so it will be accepted on your behalf; the priest is to wave it on the day after the Sabbath. On the day you wave the sheaf, you must sacrifice as a burnt offering to the LORD a lamb a year old without defect."'
> (Leviticus 23:9–12)

Here, the firstfruits, or 'first grain' is the first part of a full agricultural crop to be harvested, and it was used with symbolic force in this old covenant ritual as a means of acknowledging God as the giver of the blessing of abundant food. For the present purposes, it is most important to note that the sheaf of firstfruits was representative of the harvest as a whole. The people were not celebrating the gift of just the single bundle that the priest held aloft, but of the entire crop that the sheaf signalled. And in 1 Corinthians, Paul is likening Christ to this sheaf.

Christ appeared to many people in his resurrection partly as an indication that there was an entire harvest of similarly resurrected people to follow. That is, his resurrection was the firstfruits of the 'harvest' of the general resurrection of all of his people from the dead. And so close is this connection between Christ's resurrection and the general resurrection that it can even be helpful not to think of them as two separate events but as a single event spread out over time: Christ as the start of the harvest, his followers as the rest of the harvest, but together part of the one great harvest of the same crop. This means that the final eschatological ingathering of new resurrected people – with restored and reunified bodies and souls and transformed spiritual physicalities – has already begun in Christ, and it will be completed on the last day.

In 1 Corinthians 15:22, Paul says, 'For as in Adam all die, so in Christ all will be made alive.' He goes on in verse 49 of the same chapter, 'And just as we have borne the image of the earthly man, so shall we bear the image of the heavenly man,' underscoring that Christ's resurrection established resurrection as the pattern of future human experience in a similar way as Adam set the template for all humanity that would follow him.[9] We can add to these verses Paul's words in Philippians 3:21, which says that Christ 'will transform our lowly bodies so that they will be like his glorious body'. This is another stunning New Testament teaching that everything that was seen to be true of Christ in his resurrection will be true for his followers when he returns. And of course, none of this would be so if Christ was not fully and truly human. He would not then be the 'firstfruits' of the same kind of crop as that which will follow; he would be something else. Like the raised sheaf, his resurrection signals that there is a great deal more of the same yet to be brought in. For his resurrection to showcase the future of nature and progress of humanity, Christ has to be one of us.

Perhaps one reason that we do not always make this connection is because, although Paul explores it at length in 1 Corinthians 15, it is not included in his tight gospel summary of verses 3b–5a. In fact, it is at this point that the tight parallelism of this summary breaks down a little. Recall that we had laid out these verses in this way:

[The gospel is]	
that Christ died for our sins	– *1st part of the gospel*
in accordance with the Scriptures,	– *Fulfilling the OT*
and that he was buried,	– *There was evidence*
and	
that he has been raised on the third day	– *2nd part of the gospel*
in accordance with the Scriptures,	– *Fulfilling the OT*
and that he appeared	– *There was evidence*

But as neat as the pairing is here between the two parts of the gospel, there is in fact a difference between the ways the main verbs are qualified in their presentations. Whereas the assertion of the death of Jesus is followed by the purpose clause 'for our sins', the statement about his being raised is followed by the temporal marker 'on the third day'. This means that in Paul's gospel summary, there is no time stamp given to his death (which is significant, being on the Sabbath eve, at Passover, and possibly in the Year of Jubilee), and there is no purpose given for the resurrection.[10] Paul's summary could be filled in a little more in order to make the two statements completely parallel. Perhaps it could say

[The gospel is]
that Christ died *at Passover* for our sins
in accordance with the Scriptures,
and that he was buried,
and
that he has been raised on the third day *as the firstfruits of those who have died*
in accordance with the Scriptures,
and that he appeared

A likely reason that Paul's gospel does not have this form is simply because the earliest Christians placed a particular importance on the purpose of Jesus' death and the timing of his resurrection. This was certainly needed, at least in the case of the Corinthian church. There, the believers' continuation in sin seems to have been the result of an over-realised eschatology; the false belief that followers of Jesus were somehow already fully resurrected and living a new, completely free life that was God-blessed, irrespective of what they did.[11] Practically, this allowed them to indulge their every wish and ignore the ethical challenges of continuing to live holy lives in a world that did not recognise God. The antidote to this was not only to address each sinful practice separately, as Paul does throughout his first letter to them, but also to underscore their need for a saviour and the fact that although Christ had been raised at a discrete moment in time, his followers had not been raised yet. This is one reason why in the early part of his letter, Paul says to the Corinthians, 'For I resolved to know nothing while I was with you except Jesus Christ and him crucified' (1 Corinthians 2:2). This is a reminder that they live *before* the general resurrection, when the costly and disciplined way of the cross needs to be followed, and it explains why Paul closes his letter with a detailed unpacking of the fullness of resurrection. This is a powerful way of underlining the fact that it is impossible to believe that the Corinthians were currently experiencing fully resurrected life, and that their being mistaken in this was the root of their wrong thinking that issued in so much wrong living. Moreover, this explains why Paul crisply re-articulates the gospel at this junction in the letter. It is to say that if the Corinthians had only remembered the message that was originally proclaimed to them, the gospel message of Christ's humiliation preceding his exaltation, then they would not have been so confused about the resurrection life. Paul can confirm that yes, that completely free and new life seen in Christ will also be theirs at some time in the future, but in the meantime they are to remember the need for obedient, faithful purity while trusting in their much-needed salvation from sin by the death of Jesus.

Why God needed to rise

When explaining why the divine Jesus had to rise from the dead, one first move might be to turn to Peter's speech in Acts 2 and zero in on verse 24, where he says, 'But God raised him from the dead, freeing him from the agony of death, because it was impossible for death to keep its hold on him.' This certainly attests to the necessity of Jesus' resurrection, but does it confirm that he had to be raised because he was God and God cannot stay dead? While that line of thought seems to make sense at first, it presents a number of issues. For starters, it would mean that there is some deep theological problem with God the Son staying dead for an extended period of time, but not with him dying in the first place or being truly dead for even a short while. Resolving this issue might lead back into the thinking that death for Jesus meant some kind of suspension of his existence or of his place in the Trinity, but as we have seen, these ideas would be problematic irrespective of how long death held him down. The theological question is around how God can die at all, not how he can stay dead for more than a few days. Furthermore, if it was solely his divinity that necessitated his resurrection, the question then arises as to whether resurrection is possible apart from a divine nature, something already discussed above. Again, if we only know that resurrection is possible for divine beings, then what of the general resurrection, including the resurrection of the reprobate to face judgement and condemnation? No one would argue that the resurrection of humanity at large will be because humans have a divine nature exactly like Jesus'.[12] There is therefore no definitive reason to believe that Jesus' resurrection happened only because God cannot be dead, nor because true humans cannot rise.

Another explanation for Peter's conviction that it was impossible for Jesus to remain dead is that he recognised Jesus as the fulfilment of Psalm 16:8–11, which he quotes in Acts 2:25–28. As it happens, Peter quotes verse 10 of the psalm twice, in Acts 2:27 and again in verse 31, but he introduces a subtle change as he does. The first time, more of the psalm is quoted, showing that, in its original setting, the claim 'because you [the LORD] will not abandon me to the realm of the dead, you will not let your holy one see decay' is an expression of King David's confidence in his own preservation by God. David does not expect *his* soul to be abandoned or *his* flesh to be corrupted because '[he] saw the Lord always before [him]' and 'Because [the Lord] is at [his] right hand, [he] will not be shaken' (Acts 2:25). It is only in verse 31 that Peter rephrases the verse to be about the *Messiah* not being abandoned to the realm of the dead, nor *his* body seeing decay, having immediately prior to this explained that David remained in his tomb and that the psalm is ultimately speaking prophetically of Jesus. This might seem to be a loose use of the Old Testament by Peter, but it is actually him demonstrating that the fullness of the Old Testament can only be grasped in light of the gospel. Rather than being irresponsible with the psalm, Peter is holding the light of Jesus over it to reveal its final meaning. In Acts 13, Paul makes exactly the same point from exactly the same text. Again referencing Psalm 16, here alongside Isaiah 55, he says,

> God raised him [Jesus] from the dead so that he will never be subject to decay. As God has said,
>
> 'I will give you the holy and sure blessings promised to David.'
>
> So it is also stated elsewhere:
>
> 'You will not let your holy one see decay.'
>
> Now when David had served God's purpose in his own generation, he fell asleep [died]; he was buried with his ancestors and his body decayed. But the one whom God raised from the dead did not see decay.
>
> (Acts 13:34–37)

Like Peter in Acts 2:29, Paul points out what was obvious to everyone: this psalm could not have been fulfilled in David because David remained dead, and his body did decay. However, Jesus did not remain dead, as he was the one to whom God gave the holy and sure blessings promised to David. This does not mean that David's hope for himself was in vain; he was right to expect to be resurrected. But with Peter and Paul's help, we see that the resurrection of humanity *starts with Jesus* and then comes through him to everyone else. David will be resurrected *because of Jesus* and *after the pattern of Jesus*, the firstfruits. All of this means that the point of Psalm 16:10 is not that Jesus had to rise because he was God, but that all of the Bible's resurrection promises and hopes point to him.

A better explanation of the importance of Jesus' divinity to his resurrection is that in his resurrection, Jesus is the object of all right worship. We have already looked at Christ's humiliation in the first part of the apparent Christ hymn in Philippians 2:6–8. The second half of that hymn is all about his glorification, which comes after his death in his risen life. It teaches us that it is because Jesus stepped down from heaven and was obedient to death on the cross for the sins of the world that

> Therefore God exalted him to the highest place
> and gave him the name that is above every name,
> that at the name of Jesus every knee should bow,
> in heaven and on earth and under the earth,
> and every tongue acknowledge that Jesus Christ is Lord,
> to the glory of God the Father.
> (Philippians 2:9–11)

This is to say that everyone ought to declare the lordship of Jesus, the most highly exalted one. On bended knees, we are to direct all of our praise and worship to him, and this makes compete sense in light of his fulfilment of God's great plans. But if Jesus were not God the Son, then the same call would also run directly counter to the first two of the Ten Commandments, which prohibit having any other gods besides the true God of Israel or bending the knee to any idol in the form of anything in all creation (Exodus 20:1–4). To bow like this before Jesus if he were not the true God would be to join in the sins of the people of Babylon in Daniel's day who worshipped Nebuchadnezzar's towering gold image (Daniel 3:1–7), or the Romans who worshipped their emperors as divine.

It would also be to agree with what the Jewish leadership had said of Jesus' claim to be equal to God – that it was blasphemous in the extreme (John 5:18). But if Jesus is truly God, then devout worship of him is proper and even necessary.[13] He is worthy of all praise. And the same is true in reverse: if it is proper and necessary for humans to give ultimate honour to the champion who paid the price for sin and led the way to new and eternal life, then that one also needs to be God. For if they were only human, then we would be compelled to direct our greatest praise to a mere human because all of our hope would have been met in and through a mere human. In his resurrection, Jesus had to be God the Son because it is only the living and true God who deserves to be the object of our ongoing, eternal worship, and the Scriptures call us to worship Jesus.

*

Getting Jesus right is important for lots of reasons, and the early church worked hard to understand and articulate his divine and human natures in doctrines that faithful Christians are wise and careful to preserve today. But it is also the case that it is intrinsically necessary to the gospel that it was God the incarnate Son who died and rose. If it was not, then the gospel would not have achieved everything that it did, and its message could even lead us away from God rather than to him. This is why, inseparably interwoven with atonement and eschatology, the identity of Jesus must be seen as completely central to the Christian message. There can be no gospel without the incarnate Jesus. Those who see the gospel as the plain declaration that 'Jesus is Lord' are unquestionably on to something. Jesus is not a means to an end, as could be thought if the focus were too much on what his death and resurrection achieved and not enough on him as the Lord, who in his own right deserves to receive power and wealth and wisdom and strength and honour and glory and praise and all of our worship (Revelation 5:12). But his identity as Lord and Messiah is in no way static; it is intimately bound up with his work and indeed the only means by which God's gospel plan for his world could unfold.

6

The clearly predicted and completely unexpected gospel

So far in this study, we have been working hard to give tight definitions and to argue our points closely, sometimes resting conclusions on fine distinctions and a careful reframing of the issues. This has been important to achieve our goal of getting the biblical gospel right and starting to tease out its particular theological meanings. For the remaining four chapters however, our approach will change to one that is somewhat looser, more general and exploratory, as we shift from looking squarely and closely at the gospel to considering its broader connections with and implications for wider Christian theology and ministry practice. Here, more than pushing to define passages that seal certain conclusions, we will jump between several biblical texts as we highlight fruitful areas for further thinking. This is particularly appropriate for the closing chapter on ministry, because the need for local contextualisation is so important that it is not sensible to offer more than ideas and suggestions. All good, on-the-ground ministry is localised. In the present chapter and the following two, our thinking will also be less tied down because we are engaging some sweeping themes and major theological constructions that it would be impossible to exhaust or narrowly bind to one track of interpretation. We begin now at the highest level by considering the gospel as a message that is both plainly conveyed and yet somewhat hard to grasp through the two major divisions of the Bible: the Old and New Testaments.

One gospel, two Testaments

The relationship between the Old and New Testaments is complex. There is no dispute that the connection is very close, nor that a solid knowledge of each Testament is highly important to a good understanding of the other. By some estimates, the New Testament draws on the Old some 2,500 times. Whatever the exact number, this frequent referencing is enough to demonstrate not only that that the New Testament writers believed that what they were recording was intrinsically related to the existing Jewish religion and world-view, but also that it is sensible to find the continuation and completion of the Old Testament teachings in the story and message of Jesus. In addition to the many general works on biblical hermeneutics and exegesis that delve into the nature of the relationship between the two major divisions of the Bible, there are also countless detailed and extensive studies into the different particular ways that the Old and New Testaments interface. These include explorations of the nature and fulfilment of Old Testament prophecy in the New (sometimes including double or multiple fulfilments); the patterning, typology and recapitulations that can be observed running over the canon of Scripture; the potential for hidden meanings in the Old Testament and their revelation in the New Testament, including the possibility of *sensus plenior* (a later-revealed, fuller sense); the thousands of cross-Testamental connections noted above; and even the ways that Jesus might or might not have been the person of the Trinity who was manifested in the Old Testament theophanies.[1] Good work in all of these areas is absolutely essential to proper interpretation of the Bible and it often requires us, appropriately, to look at the completed text of Scripture from outside of its unfolding story and to bring in important insights and wisdom from literary and historical research, as well as considerations and observations from standard biblical studies and systematic theology. As thankful as we are for all of this labour, it can additionally be helpful to narrow down and explore the relationship of the Testaments from within the perspective of Bible's own unfolding narrative and especially from the viewpoint of those who first, and perhaps therefore most acutely, felt the challenge of bringing the established Jewish beliefs into harmony with the person, works and message of Jesus. There is value in trying to stand in the place of the peoples who actually lived through the times and events recorded in the New Testament, at that monumental turning of the theological ages, in order to mentally and even emotionally enter into the moment when God was rolling out his gospel work and its first proclamation. This posture allows us to get some sense of how those who first encountered the gospel saw the relationship between it and the well-established Jewish faith out of which it arose. It is from this place that we might be best able to see how the gospel is both the completely natural and the best possible culmination of so much that is found in the Old Testament, while being at exactly the same time significantly out of step with so many of the common contemporary expectations for God's next moves among his people.

The broad substance of the connections between Jesus and the old covenant people of God are obvious enough. Jesus himself was of course completely and unashamedly Jewish. He was born and lived in first-century Jewish Palestine. He consciously held the Jewish peoples and their Scripture based faith as his first interest and as foundational to his personal identity and mission. And he took Israel's history as his own, right from its ultimate ancestry in Adam and Eve, through the patriarchs, on to the establishment of the geopolitical nation first under Moses and later under successive kings ruling from Jerusalem, all the way to the exile into Babylon and the return of the remnant people to rebuild. Jesus even identified with the intertestamental history of Israel, when Greece and then Rome were the dominant powers under which God's people had been variously subdued and compromised. Even those who today reject Jesus as central to the continuation of God's plans do not contest that his story was squarely set in the story of the Jewish people and nation.

As much as these observations are basic, it is also obvious that there are many ways in which Jesus and his message mark some notable discontinuities from what came before. Like any great story, the Bible's grand narrative has plot twists and unexpected disjunctures that intrigue us as readers just as they challenged the minds and hearts of those who lived through them. If Jesus was who he said he was, and if his message was true, then many of the first-century people who sought to be faithful to God would have needed to readjust their world-view in some most substantial ways. One important example of this, which is shot right through the New Testament, has to do with the place of non-Jewish peoples among the people of God. While there had always been people from other ethnic and political communities who joined in Israel's worship, their social, cultural and racial distance from the centre of the Jewish peoples meant that they remained marked out in some significant ways, including being restricted to the outer court of the Gentiles when visiting the Jerusalem temple.[2] If any of these God-fearers did want to fully and formally commit to the Jewish religion and nation, then they had to submit to the regulations of Jewish law, which included the prescriptions for Sabbathing, dietary restrictions and circumcision for men. But Jesus and the apostles ended all of this, as they called and welcomed people from all nations and backgrounds to worship in spirit and truth and recast all of the requirements of the law in the process, including those for the Sabbath, the old food laws and circumcision.[3] This was radical grace for those Gentiles who came to Christ, and it demanded a radical mental and social reset for his Jewish followers.

While the example of Gentile inclusion is clear enough (although still without any unanimity among scholars in its details), in some cases, the nature and degree of the potential continuities and discontinuities between the Testaments are more hotly debated. For example, there are some who argue that the coming of Jesus did not change the spiritual importance of an ethnic and geopolitical Israel. Indeed, some current versions of dispensationalist theology still champion the idea that Israel as a theocratic, temporal nation-state remains very much at the forefront of God's plans for his world today, in contrast to others who see the people of God established in that way as only the Old Testament precursor to the worldwide, multiethnic body of the Christian church.[4] There is also the question of whether Jesus changed the Old Testament's system of a works-based righteousness grounded in God's law to a grace-based righteousness grounded in faith, or whether salvation by grace through faith is constant between both Testaments, and the real difference is that the New Testament calls for salvation by grace through faith in the particular person of Jesus.[5]

We will not attempt to engage the detail of these issues here, much less offer any resolutions to them. There are already many weighty volumes that delve deeply into them all, and many more too. We only raise them to highlight that, even though the details of the relationship can be much debated, all mainstream Christians agree that the New Testament is both a continuation with and a departure from the Old, and that the same is the case for the gospel itself.

In the rest of this chapter, we will note some of the ways that Jesus' identity as the God-man, his death for sins and his resurrection as the firstfruits of the new creation all beautifully fulfil and simultaneously confound the pre-existing expectations of many of the Jews of his day. As we now take a more narratival approach, we remember our earlier observation that this is the way that some scholars seek out and identify the gospel message. Although we concluded that this might not be the surest way to crystallise a sharp gospel definition, we can still recognise that it is the best way to grasp the dynamic of the gospel as it is announced in the context of the established Old Testament faith. Each approach yields its own benefits. There is also a possibility that once we have recognised some of the major continuities and discontinuities between the Old Testament-based beliefs of many of the Jews in Jesus' day and the New Testament with its gospel message, we might then have a little more light to guide us through some of the more contentious questions of continuity and discontinuity flagged above. But giving thought to this dynamic of retaining but reframing will at least lead to a very practical conclusion related to the church's mandate to proclaim the gospel, which we will come to at the end of the chapter. Once more, our aim is not to catalogue every way in which the gospel both flows seamlessly from the Old Testament and at the same time turns the common understanding of it upside down. Rather, we will take a few choice examples to demonstrate that it certainly does both of those things.

Messiah

There are many Old Testament texts that the New Testament interprets as relating to Jesus as the Messiah, the Son of the living God. Famous among these are Matthew 1:22–23, referring back to Isaiah 7:14's prediction of the birth of one to be called Immanuel, meaning 'God with us'; Hebrews 1:5, which claims that God's declaration in Psalm 2:7 that he is Father to a Son was specifically fulfilled in Jesus; and Luke 3:3–6, where John the Baptist is identified as the one who would prepare the way for the Lord as written in Isaiah 40:3–5.

As familiar as these connections now are to Christian readers of the Bible, it was perhaps not unambiguously clear that the first-century Jews were awaiting a messianic fulfilment of each of these Old Testament texts. For example, many would have thought that in foretelling the birth of an Immanuel, Isaiah was speaking of his own son – who is mentioned in Isaiah 8:1–4 – and so they would not have necessarily been awaiting any other child to fulfil the prophet's words. This means that the bare fact of Matthew presenting Isaiah's text as a prophecy that had finally been fulfilled would have wrong-footed many of those who first read his Gospel, irrespective of how, or by whom, Matthew believed that the prophecy had only recently come to pass. This example shows us that one reason that the gospel often confounded the common expectations of its day was not because it cut against them, but simply because it made some very significant claims where there were in fact no specific expectations whatsoever. It is one thing to be surprised by an unexpected resolution to a known issue; it is another to be presented with a resolution when no issue was recognised in the first place. We will see the same when we come to the death and resurrection of Jesus: some of the New Testament's interpretations of those events in the context of the Old spoke into a general silence on the topics rather than eager expectations. (Incidentally, this 'answering a question that no one was asking' might also explain the existence of some of the above-mentioned debates around continuity of Old Testament ideas into the New. If no change was expected to, say, the geopolitical status of Israel, then an unexpected change might not only take some people's understanding in a new direction, but might also lead others to refuse the legitimacy of any change whatsoever.)

However, in addition to these sorts of cases, there are also many Old Testament passages that do directly and unambiguously predict the coming of a new divine messiah figure and which therefore would have been the loci of that conscious expectation for first-century Jews who were actively awaiting their fulfilment. Example passages are:

- 2 Samuel 7:12–15, which predicts a king who will rise up in the line of David to reign forever.
- Psalm 110:1–2, which reports God addressing a 'lord' of David who will sit at God's right hand and suppress his enemies.

- Isaiah 9:6–7, which speaks of a son born to carry the government of David's kingdom eternally while bearing multiple divine titles.
- Ezekiel 37:24, which foretells a future David who will rule over the reunited kingdoms of Israel and Judah.
- Micah 5:2–5, where a ruler will arise from Bethlehem to shepherd his flock in the name and strength of God and whose greatness will reach to the ends of the earth.
- Zechariah 9:9–10, which calls Jerusalem to rejoice in the king who will arrive riding on the colt of a donkey and who will rule in peace to the ends of the earth.

Aspects of Micah and Zechariah's prophecies were plainly met by Jesus in the setting of his birth and his triumphal entry into Jerusalem (Luke 2:1–7, 19:28–40). For anyone who knew those parts of his story, suggesting that Jesus was the fulfilment of the prophets' words would have been at least plausible. For those who would accept him, the other texts were equally fulfilled by Jesus as the true king of the Jews. But of course, many did not accept him because his way of being the Jewish messiah did not marry up with the presumptions that so many had had regarding the coming of God's ruler to his throne. For them, Simon Maccabeus – one of the Jewish leaders of the intertestamental period who defended Jerusalem and finally expelled the Syrians who had occupied the citadel – was maybe closer to the mark. That story is recorded in 1 Maccabees, an apocryphal text that was important to the national history of Israel in the first century:

> Those [Syrians] who were in the citadel at Jerusalem were prevented [by Simon] from going in and out to buy and sell in the country. So they were very hungry, and many of them perished from famine. Then they cried to Simon to make peace with them, and he did so. But he expelled them from there and cleansed the citadel from its pollutions. On the twenty-third day of the second month, in the one hundred and seventy-first year, the Jews entered it with praise and palm branches, and with harps and cymbals and stringed instruments, and with hymns and songs, because a great enemy had been crushed and removed from Israel. Simon decreed that every year

> they should celebrate this day with rejoicing. He strengthened the fortifications of the temple hill alongside the citadel, and he and his men lived there.
> (1 Maccabees 13:49–52 NRSV)

Here a great military leader of the Jews rids the holy city of foreigners before his people enter in waving palm branches and singing songs of praise and celebration. Simon then reinforces the citadel and takes up residence there. There are some undeniable echoes of this as Jesus rides into Roman-occupied Jerusalem to the acclaim of the crowd, who are also waving palm branches and joyfully acknowledging him as their God-given Saviour (Luke 19:28–40). But Jesus does not get rid of Jerusalem's occupiers, nor strengthen the city, nor settle in as ruler. Instead, in the eyes of the crowd, his 'triumphal' entry ends up being a huge anticlimax, which results in his death and no immediately observable benefits for them. He cannot have been king of the Jews after all, and the sign that hangs over him as he is crucified (John 19:19) is a cruel irony. Except that, for those who received his word, it is a double irony because he really was the king of the Jews, but he could only be recognised as such by those willing to let their assumptions about kingship be challenged and for his reign and rule to be radically different from that which they had anticipated.

He did not come to defeat the Romans but sin and Satan. He did not come to free the people from military oppression but spiritual oppression. He did not come to take up a worldly throne but a heavenly one (John 18:36). He perfectly fulfilled what the Old Testament predicted, and yet it happened in ways that were completely unexpected by so many who had latched onto a different interpretation of the biblical hope.

Death

This same alignment with the course of the Old Testament and simultaneous deviation from the hopes of so many people who sought to live by it, is clear when considering Jesus' death and its accomplishments. Probably the most important example of this is found in the ways that Jesus' death fulfils Isaiah 52:13–53:12, the last of Isaiah's so-called Servant

Songs. This passage speaks at some length about a coming servant who will be raised up and exalted but also despised and rejected. It speaks of him being plain in appearance – not impressively tall like King Saul nor especially good looking like King David (1 Samuel 10:23–24; 16:12) – and says that although pure and innocent, he would be treated like a criminal by the people around him and would also end up taking on the wrath of God due to humanity for its faithlessness. Indeed, in the language of the sacrificial system, God would make his life an offering for sin (Isaiah 53:10). But at the end of the passage, Isaiah says that he would be vindicated and given a portion among the great (Isaiah 53:12).

Several things are interesting about this text. First, in the first century, it was clearly awaiting a fulfilment. Unlike the prediction in Isaiah 7 of a coming Immanuel, there was no common view that what was foretold had already come to pass. This was something that God's people were still looking forward to. Second, most of the writers of the New Testament directly quote a part of it (and thereby often infer or assume the whole) as being fulfilled in Jesus and his atoning death.[6] Mark does not quote the passage, but many commentators believe that it was in Jesus' mind when he made his programmatic statement, 'For even the Son of Man did not come to be served, but to serve, and to give his life as a ransom for many' (Mark 10:45).[7] With this level of attention given to the passage in the New Testament, it is indisputable that the earliest proclaimers of the gospel thought that it was highly significant to their message. Third, however, is the fact that the passage itself predicts the mixed reception that would greet the one who fulfilled it. The suffering servant would be both highly exalted and despised (Isaiah 52:13, 53:3). Presumably, his rejection would at least in part be connected to his lowly appearance and his terrible death, which would not have gelled with many peoples' ideas about the nature and experiences expected of God's greatest agents. So while many in the onlooking crowds were right to recognise that Jesus' punishment, strikings and afflictions were deserved judgements, they failed to realise that he was not the one who deserved them, and they could not square his situation with him being God incarnate. Fourth and similarly, the passage itself prophesies that the message that would later be spoken about Jesus would be received well by some but rejected by others. Some kings would understand it, but many Israelites would not believe it (Isaiah 52:15–53:1). The very fact that these Old Testament verses have such warnings written into them should have given decent pause for thought to any who would move quickly to reject Jesus as its fulfilment. They ought to have seen God's negative assessment of those who failed to see past the external appearances of the one who would be his suffering servant. And they ought to have taken the prompt to reflect on whether their own evaluation of Jesus would put them in that group.

People might have made this misjudgement of Jesus because they did not expect the messiah and the suffering servant to be the same person. That God would send a king greater than David to rule and lead was a promise that could be embraced and eagerly waited upon. So too was the hope that the people's sins would be borne away by a sacrificial saviour. But the suggestion that these two were one would have thrown out the national expectations that had been built up over the centuries. Once more, the sign hung above Christ on the cross was challenging, as it brought together Christ's kingship and his suffering – things that were very hard to mentally reconcile, especially in that moment. Surely God's promised king could not die such a death. Surely God's promised sacrifice would not be made by his long-anticipated greatest king.

In addition to the particular text of Isaiah's prophecy being obviously but unexpectedly met in the death of King Jesus, we can also note that the wider New Testament, particularly the book of Hebrews, takes Jesus' death as the culmination and conclusion of the Old Testament sacrificial system as a whole. Unlike Isaiah 52:13–53:12, this is another example of the gospel recapitulating and completing something from Israel's past for which the first-century Jewish people were not necessarily expecting any fresh developments. Looking backwards, it is not difficult to see how the sacrificial system was ultimately inadequate, and how Jesus' death fully and finally accomplished what it never could. But looking forward with Old Testament eyes, it might not have been so apparent.

Hebrews 9 explains that the tabernacle (and by extension the temple) was not beyond improvement as it was made by human hands, itself needed cleansing, and was set up for sacrifices that needed to be offered repeatedly and received a priest who did not offer the greatest sacrifice of his own blood. We even learn that this tabernacle and the entire set of rituals that took place in it were mere copies of the true sanctuary of heaven, which is far superior. The cleansing that happens in the heavenly sanctuary is not just external; it is achieved by one single pure sacrifice, the effects of which are sufficient for all of God's people forever. That sacrifice was Jesus the Messiah. The first half of Hebrews chapter 10 goes on to underscore and reinforce that the sacrificial system only ever foreshadowed the coming of Christ and that the repetition of sacrifices proves their ultimate ineffectiveness. It even states bluntly, 'It is impossible for the blood of bulls and goats to take away sins' (Hebrews 10:4). Parts of this are obvious, even for those deeply embedded in the routines and practices of the temple. A goat is not an adequate exchange for a human being. A solution that needs to be implemented over and over again is not a lasting solution. A ritual can be enacted without having any impact on the conscience. Even so, it is still neither immediately obvious to conclude nor easy to accept that a human being – let alone God's Messiah, let alone the incarnate God-man – would be needed to accomplish once and for all what a system that had stood for well over a thousand years ultimately could not. Although foreshadowed in many ways, this aspect of the gospel is still unexpected. It requires great humility and a considerable reconfiguration of accepted thought to receive. But when it is accepted, it makes complete sense of all that came before.

Resurrection

Moving finally to Jesus' resurrection, the same pattern can be found: in many ways it meets the hopes and expectations of the Old Testament, but in others it requires quite new or refreshed thinking. One of the great images of resurrection in the Old Testament is the vision of the dry bones in Ezekiel 37:1–14. This passage gives a graphic description of resurrection with the prophet first being led through a valley floor covered by many completely dried up human bones before God asks him whether those bones can live again. After deferring to God's knowledge on the matter, Ezekiel is instructed to call the bones back to life, and he watches as they rejoin. Tendons reconnect, flesh is filled out and skin covers over. Although this is all quite incredible, the restored bodies remain lifeless at this point. But then, there is a second move that is reminiscent of Genesis 2:7, where God breathed the breath of life into the body of Adam, whom he had just formed from dust. Ezekiel is directed to call the breath of life into the re-formed bodies, which he does, and that breath again comes and brings life, with the result that the army of once-dead people then rise to their feet.

As much as this is a powerful image of the general resurrection for New Testament readers, in the first place, this vision is not given to Ezekiel as a promise of resurrection at all. Rather, it is an illustration of Israel's restoration to their homeland after the exile (Ezekiel 36:16–38). The image of the 'very dry' bones is a striking way of showing just how spiritually dead God's people were when they were removed from the place where they had experienced his particular presence and been blessed with lives that were structured around faithful worship. Watching those bones returned to full, healthy and functional life is a vivid picture of the power of God to do the most impossible things, particularly giving sure hope of the end of exile and a return to a blessed life in the promised land with hearts set right before God. However, the illustration in Ezekiel is not completely arbitrary; it secondarily points to the even greater hope of eternal life spent in the presence of God. As it turned out, the restoration of the exiles to the land was not a return to the glory days of King David but to occupation and oppression first by Hellenics under Alexander the Great and then by Rome. Poverty, hardships and death remained a constant reality for God's people in his land, and in that context, the people did look forward to a post-mortem hope. The development of this hope can be traced through the intertestamental literature, but it also tracks back to Old Testament texts like Ezekiel 37:1–14 and Daniel 12:2–3.[8] Thus, by Jesus' time, the Pharisees – a leading Jewish group with both scholarly and political interests – were known for their belief in the resurrection, a contrast to their political rivals the Sadducees who did not share that conviction (Acts 23:8). Hope in resurrection is also openly expressed to Jesus by Martha of Bethany when they are at the tomb of her brother Lazarus (John 11:21–24), and this shows its wider diffusion among more common people too.

Given all of this, the resurrection of Jesus would seem to very clearly meet the conscious hopes of many of the Jewish people who first heard about it as a central part of the gospel message. And yet once more, there was too much about it that was unexpected and made it hard to reconcile straightforwardly with the prevailing expectations. We have already seen that it took some time for everyone who encountered Jesus in his resurrection body to be convinced that it really was him. Whatever the physical details, the transformation that accompanied his resurrection initially seemed to conceal that he was the same person who had died three days earlier.[9] And so, while some took the identification of Jesus as the risen one to be the central and motivating factor for their evangelism, others might have found the reports of a fantastical transformation to be a barrier to believing that the resurrection had begun. After all, the visions of Ezekiel 37 and Daniel 12 do not obviously include anything that would lead to the belief that risen people are physically changed. Even the Daniel text's prediction of the resurrected shining 'like the brightness of the heavens' and 'like the stars for ever and ever' (Daniel 12:3) could understandably be taken as metaphors for a new moral holiness, spiritual purity and eternal life such that both passages can fairly be read as anticipating resurrection only as a straightforward physical restoration, not a transformation.[10]

Beyond this is also the fact that Jesus rose alone as the firstfruits, not as part of a great resurrection of everyone who had died. From the perspective of the Old Testament, this meant that the resurrection hope, which had reasonably been thought to be arriving in a single moment, needed to be re-understood as an event that had always sat on a hidden double horizon with Jesus first and his followers later, something that many had not been looking for at all. Thus, the claim that Jesus' rising was a legitimate fulfilment of the Old Testament predictions of resurrection even though it was separated from the general resurrection required a major mental recalibration.

As it turns out, the delayed timing of the general resurrection caused a breadth of concerns and confusion in the early church. We know that this troubled the Thessalonians, who were worried that those who had died in the faith while waiting for Jesus' return had somehow missed out on the eternity that he had promised. Paul assured them that this was not at all the case, that the general resurrection, although some time after Jesus' resurrection, was still to come and that the Christian departed would certainly be part of it. Indeed, he taught that the dead would in fact rise to be with Christ first (1 Thessalonians 4:13–18). And as we have seen, the Corinthians seem to have assumed that they must have already experienced some kind of resurrection into a new free life, a belief that Paul strongly put down, pressing the same point that the general resurrection is still to come.[11]

The chronological gap between Christ's resurrection and his return to judge at the time of general resurrection ought not to have been a surprise to anyone familiar with the teaching of Jesus found in texts such as Matthew 24 and 25. After speaking about some of the events surrounding the time of his return, Jesus says that no one knows the day or the hour that these things will occur (Matthew 24:36). However, he then proceeds to tell a number of parables that, in stepwise fashion, lay out the way his people should think about the timing of his return. First, he recalls the suddenness of the arrival of the flood in the days of Noah and speaks of a house owner needing to be prepared for a break-in at all times lest the thief comes when they are being inattentive (Matthew 24:37–44). The same message is found in the next parable about a master who returns unexpectedly from a time away and catches his lead servant abusing his fellow servants rather than feeding and caring for them as he had been called to do (Matthew 24:45–51). The simple lesson from these two parables is that Christ could return at any time, so his people always need to be faithful and watchful. The parable of the ten virgins follows, and it thickens this lesson up by showing that part of being ever-ready involves being ready for what could be a long wait (Mathew 25:1–13). The virgins who did not bring spare oil for their lamps were not prepared for such a long wait and ended up missing out on the groom's arrival, as they were distracted by the need to go off and resupply. Their short-range thinking cost them dearly. So we see that while Jesus taught that he could return at any time, he also told us that he might not return for a long time. The last parable of the sequence does not add any more to the question of when Jesus might return or when the general resurrection would occur, but it points to the need for his people to be active and productive in his affairs while they are waiting (Matthew 25:14–30).

The sad thing about all of these parables is that they acknowledge the very real possibility that some people will not be waiting appropriately for Jesus' return in light of his resurrection and in hope of their own.

Even though resurrection meets the ultimate and eternal hope of the Old Testament, there were many expectations that its nature and timing did not quickly match. It was plainly predicted, but it confounded many who were faced with it.

Acceptance of Christ's resurrection continues to be a stumbling block to today's secular modernists, although their objection is not around its nature or timing, but just that such a thing is fundamentally impossible. Sadly, too many who are not Christian, yet who would love a sure hope for something secure after death, fail to see that the Christian gospel directly meets that hope in the shape of biblical resurrection, with Christ's resurrection as its paradigm. Like many in the first century, the good news sounds good, but it often remains too jarring to be welcomed as life-giving truth.

The need for gospel proclamation and the Holy Spirit

Much of this chapter might seem interesting and yet not directly relevant to contemporary Christian life, except perhaps to the work of evangelising adherents to Judaism whose Scriptures Christians take as their Old Testament. However, there are three very important general truths here that ought to shape all of our evangelistic efforts. The first is that Jesus meets the greatest and deepest needs and wants of everyone, even when these have not been clearly identified or when they have been cast very differently. At root, everyone wants to have knowledge of divine truth. Some look for this in the mainstream religions, some in alternative or bespoke spiritualities. Even staunch atheists want this in the sense that they feel that it is important to them to shape their lives around the belief that there is no god. Similarly, almost everyone wants to feel at peace with the divine and at peace with others. No religions, spiritualities or philosophies trade on the promise of rejection or conflict with the gods or fellow humans; they all offer their adherents some form of rightness with the world and whatever spiritual powers might oversee it, even if there are trials to be faced along the way. And everyone wants a good life and hopes for security and good things in the future. It could be argued that nihilistic or suicidal people do not want these things, but the fact that most nihilists do not commit suicide shows that they have things that they still want from life, and it is the great sadness of suicide that those who consider it or commit it do not do so from anything like their own preferred physical, mental, emotional or spiritual place. While being conscious of the sensitivities of different people's personal situations and the huge variety of forms that individuals' hopes can take, it is clear that the gospel of Jesus has something to offer everyone not only in a fundamental or abstract sense, but also at the level of their felt needs. (One of the great challenges for evangelism today is finding the intersection of people's felt needs and the truths of the gospel. This requires a lot of listening and curbing of any impulses to make quick and simplistic connections. The same is in fact true for the work of pastoring believers.) The gospel meets our deepest longings today just as it met many of the expectations of the first-century Jews living in Palestine who were the first to hear it.

The second thing is that the gospel does not always meet people's needs in ways that they would anticipate or that they immediately want. It does not help us to get in touch with the divine by 'being true to ourselves' as that idea is commonly cast today. Rather, it connects us with the divine by showing us that Jesus is God with us, and by calling us to be true to him.[12] The gospel does not offer us God's acceptance and peace with others by having us prove ourselves worthy, nor by validating our every impulse, but by bringing us to acknowledge the ways that we fall short and the ways that we have done and been wrong. It brings atonement through honesty and humility, not through success and indiscriminate affirmation. And the gospel does not give life and justice and other good things through a health programme, a judicial tribunal, a promise of temporal prosperity or even the end to global conflict, but through hope beyond the grave. The new and renewed life and world that we wish for is one that ultimately only comes on the other side of death, not one that will ever be completely realised now, even as we give thanks for daily graces. In the gospel, there is a challenge for believers to embrace the new life fully by letting go of many of their present aspirations and securities. It is challenging to help to enlighten those who do not recognise that their needs can only be met in such unpredictable ways. Just as the gospel confounded the expectations of its earliest audiences and so needed to be expounded at length in their time, both its content and its unexpectedness continue to need to be unpacked today.

It is important to say at this point that there is a dark side to the project of explaining the gospel and the ways that it meets the deepest human needs and longings. So far in this chapter, the gospel has been presented as a message that is as confounding and unexpected as it is fulfilling. But casting it in this way can make it sound as though the only challenge it brings is intellectual or paradigmatic, as though fresh thinking is all that is needed for the gospel to be embraced. While this might sometimes be the case, it is also very true that many people reject the gospel because of deep seated pride and because of its moral implications. In Romans 1:18–32, a weighty passage of the Bible, Paul explains that the human problem is not ultimately a lack of knowledge, but that wicked people suppress the truth and do not seek to honour God even though they know at least something of him. Rather, their priority is serving their own creatureliness, even with all of its worst desires and distorted thoughts that lead to all forms of immorality.

In short, much of humanity's issue lies not in an inability to understand the gospel, but in the choice to reject God and the knowledge that his ways are good and right. Similarly, the Pharisees who interacted with Jesus were not intellectually limited such that they could not stretch their thinking to conceive of a different way of putting the story of God's people together. Rather, their problems were more tied up with power and pride. Throughout the Gospels, we see that their problem was not in their heads but in their hearts. Having a backwater peasant call them to let go of their approach to the Scriptures, their understanding of God and his work in the world and their own comfortable place within all of that was too much for them. Before they could accept the gospel with all of its fresh paradigms, they needed humble and penitent hearts. They needed to be *willing* as well as *thinking* in their approach to Jesus. They needed to want to approach him, not just understand him. This required a work of the Holy Spirit.

One of the most unexpected things that Jesus says comes in John 16:7. There, he tells his disciples that it is for their good that he is going away – that is, it will be good for them when he leaves the earth to return to his Father in heaven, something that he discusses right across John's Gospel.

But how could it be of great benefit for Jesus to leave his people? Surely they would be better off if he stayed at their side always. And surely their mission of proclaiming the gospel would benefit from his continued presence too. Imagine for a moment how helpful it would be for world evangelisation if Jesus had never ascended back into heaven. It would be ridiculously easy for us to declare that we had the secret to eternal life if our leader was still walking the earth after 2,000 years! But Jesus did not see it that way. He thought that it was to his followers' advantage for him to leave. His reasoning was that if he did not go away, then the Advocate, the Spirit, would not come, but if he did go, then he could send him. For some reason beyond what has been revealed to us, the coming of the Holy Spirit required Jesus to be in heaven to send him. And while the mechanics of that remain opaque to us, it turns the question to why Jesus thought it would be better for the Spirit than the Son to be present with us.

We get something of the answer from Jesus' words in the next verse of John 16. Here we learn that 'when [the Spirit] comes, he will prove the world to be in the wrong about sin and righteousness and judgement' (John 16:8), although this can also be fairly rendered as 'he will convict the world about sin and righteousness and judgement.' The term 'convict' is perhaps a more helpful translation of the underlying Greek than 'prove wrong', as it indicates a change of heart, not just a defeat in an argument. It shows that the Spirit has a special role in working to alter internally held beliefs in ways that external evidence cannot. It might be useful at this point to think of Jesus as God's more 'natural' presence, interacting with people's senses and minds as he spoke of and demonstrated the truths of the gospel to the world, and of the Holy Spirit as God's more 'supernatural' presence, interacting with people's souls and wills in ways that are imperceptible, unpredictable and beyond human resistance.[13] (Although it must be flagged that while this framing can sometimes be helpful for our thinking, it can also be unhelpful at other times.) It is a sad reality that many people who interacted with Jesus in the flesh still ended up rejecting him. Despite his miracles, his wisdom, his irrefutable teachings and his perfect and loving character, they still refused to follow him. This is because his divinity was communicated within his humanity, and some people never saw past the humanity. But when the Spirit engages a person, God is working directly on their hearts such that they can come to belief even without ever having seen or talked with Jesus (cf. John 20:29). Paul captures something of this idea in relation to the reception of the gospel in 1 Thessalonians, where he writes,

> For we know, brothers and sisters loved by God, that he has chosen you, because our gospel came to you not simply with words but also with power, with the Holy Spirit and deep conviction.
> (1 Thessalonians 1:4–5a)

The gospel was received by the Thessalonians not just because Paul and others had done so well at explaining its fulfilling and unexpected nature to them in words, but also because of the inner working of the Holy Spirit that was tied up with their becoming convicted of its truth. As much as we must labour to keep understanding and sharing the natural and radical message of the gospel, in the end, our faith in Jesus is a gift of the Spirit. As important as it is, understanding is not always a sure pathway to faith because human pride and stubbornness can still stand in the way.

Even having said all of this, our third and final point is that it is still the case that the gospel must be told, taught and explained because the Spirit's work of softening and converting hearts is often coupled with fuller understanding. Theologically, we say that the gospel is a truth of special revelation, not general revelation. This means that the gospel is in no way made obvious from observation of the world around us, nor is it deductible from other knowledge that we might have. It is not something that anyone could conclude after reflection or that could be arrived at through any series of logical calculations. We certainly cannot expect people to pick up the gospel only by observing the moral behaviour of Christians absent of any declaration of the message itself; observing moral behaviour is more likely to promote the value of being a good person, not being a saved sinner. To be sure, there is a certain logic to the gospel as there is to much of Christian belief and Christian ethics, and lots of modern-day Christian apologetics seeks to demonstrate all of this. But the core truths about the identity of Jesus as Messiah, his death that brings atonement and his resurrection that leads to full and eternal life are also profoundly counter-intuitive and non-intuitive. As such, they can usually only be known if they are heard or read, and that means that God's people must make it their priority to share the gospel proactively and explicitly. As Paul puts it,

> 'Everyone who calls on the name of the Lord will be saved.'
> How, then, can they call on the one they have not believed in? And how can they believe in the one of whom they have not heard? And how can they hear without someone preaching to them? And how can anyone preach unless they are sent? As it is written: 'How beautiful are the feet of those who bring good news!'
> (Romans 10:13–15)

In chapter 9, we will think more about the gospel and Christian ministry. Next, however, we turn to explore more of the connections between the gospel and the breadth of Christian theology.

7
The gospel and gospel theology

So far, we have argued that the surest way to arrive at a dependable definition of the gospel is through exegesis of the short biblical text that most unambiguously articulates it: 1 Corinthians 15:3b–5a. Looking at this text confirmed for us that the gospel is the message of the death and resurrection of the Messiah, and we found that it is important to understand both the events of the gospel and the theological meaning of those events in some detail. We also found that it was critical for Jesus to be both fully God and fully man, in line with the historic orthodox claims of Christianity, in order for the gospel to be effective. Then, in the previous chapter, we noted how this message of the dying and rising of the divine-human completely fulfilled many of the hopes of the people to whom he first came and yet was also profoundly unexpected. All of this amounts to decent coverage and a fair thickening up of a good, basic understanding of the central Christian message. Now, we come to expand our thinking further to consider something more of the relationship of the gospel to the fuller body of Christian theology.

While there are strong, natural and vital connections to be demonstrated here, they are not nowadays made as often as they ought to be, and they are not at all clear to many rank and file Christians. This might be because, on the one hand, the gospel is often thought about as just the straightforward, stand-alone message of the faith proclaimed by evangelists and church leaders to non-Christians in the hope that they will accept it and so receive new life in Jesus. Come to Jesus for forgiveness, hope, identity and purpose – simple. On the other hand, systematic theology is commonly perceived to be a largely academic discipline that takes professors and seminary students through complex, technical and abstract subjects that are relatively opaque to most regular believers who do not understand much about them or see much of their relevance. How does knowing the difference between supralapsarianism and infralapsarianism impact what we are going to do at church this Sunday, let alone what we do through the rest of the week? When put like this, both the unacceptability of the disjuncture and the truth behind the caricatures is obvious. Beyond this, it is also the case that even within the academy, the gospel is often treated as though it were one theological topic among many, and it is not standard practice to begin a course of doctrinal study or to start an investigation of a theological topic through the lens of the gospel, nor to tie other areas of Christian thought back to the gospel or its theology routinely. Yet things ought not to be this way. First, the gospel must be received as more than the gateway into Christianity through which converts pass before essentially leaving it behind as they shift their attention to other priorities such as personal morality, social order, church life or even higher theological studies. Instead, the gospel must be understood as the constant centrepiece and definer of every part of the Christian experience. Christians should be lifelong gospel people, and that does not only mean people who are always proclaiming the gospel to others (although they should be that), but also people who strive to have every thought and each piece of their lives taken captive to obey Christ and the good news about him (2 Corinthians 10:5). The maturing Christian does not ever progress past the gospel, but only goes deeper and deeper into it, being more and more transformed by it and conformed to it.[1] This is a lifelong project that actually turns out to be quite challenging, even with the indwelling of the Holy Spirit. This is at least partly because of the significant ethical transformation that the unexpected and radical nature of the gospel demands, and that resurrection people undergo. Those who receive the gospel in their hearts cannot simply return to the same ways of thinking and living that they had previously. Even if they had always been largely upright and good people who did not need a complete reorientation of their morality and behaviour, they were not 'gospel people', people whose entire perspective on life was refracted through the crystallised truths about Jesus. Certainly, no convert should return to the more merit-based patterns of relating to the world that come naturally to most humans, nor should they grow into a version of Christianity that is largely only cultural. The gospel through which they are converted should make them people who forever seek to glorify and worship Jesus the king, who offers and models healed life as grace and who gives hope beyond all concerns of this present existence. They should become people who are always acknowledging their need for God's intervention in their lives and their dependence on him for each breath they take. They should be people who keep returning to the throne, the cross and the empty tomb as their first love, their deep peace and their certain hope.

But as right as all of this is, it does not for a moment mean that there is no place for deeper theological thought or explorations. Going ever further into the breadth and details of the word of God, and into all of the questions and issues that it raises, is something that every able believer ought to do. Whereas the gospel can be boiled down to a few words and helpfully expounded over a few pages or through a few minutes of discussion, the Bible is not a short book, and neither is it an endlessly repetitive book that has nothing new to offer once the basic gospel message is grasped. It is not as though its sixty-six separate texts, made up of a total of 1,189 chapters, all just outline the gospel over and over in the same way, such that the only necessary skill in mature Bible reading is being able to find precisely the same message on every single page. Rather, God has given us such a large Bible because there is a great deal of himself and his ways and countless other truths that he wants his people to be engaged by and to grapple with. We are to plumb the depths of the Scriptures, seeking to understand and internalise as much of them as we are able to, savouring every part as we go. In short, Christians must strive to embrace the whole Bible and to do so deeply and theologically, lest they remain immature and spiritually shallow, feeding only on the milk of the faith and never getting stuck into the solid food (1 Corinthians 3:2; Hebrews 5:11–14.).

Putting these two things together – that we must remain gospel-centred people and be avid biblical theologians – makes the imperative to understand the relationship between the gospel and Christian theology clear. We must know how we can stay grounded in the gospel while at the same time constantly progressing our knowledge of the Bible and the many and diverse things that it teaches. Of course, in this book we have already begun to do this, as we have explored some of the theology undergirding and flowing from the simple gospel message. As we have considered the summary statement that the Messiah died for our sins and rose again as the firstfruits, we have tapped into Christology, soteriology and eschatology, and we have seen that we could go a lot further into these major areas of doctrine. We have also seen something of the connectedness of those different doctrines and the ways that each depends on the others to make sense and for the gospel to achieve its purpose. This is unsurprising, as the whole body of Christian theology is ultimately interrelated. While it is often split up into manageable topics for the purposes of research and study, the further we go into any area of the church's doctrine, the more we find ourselves touching on its other topics and seeing how inseparably each part of Christian belief is enmeshed with the rest.

This interrelatedness of all of the parts of Christian theology is well-known enough, and with this in mind, the purpose of the present chapter is to explore some of the ways that the whole body of theology naturally flows out of and ties back into the foundational message of the gospel. There are three closely related reasons for considering this. The first is simply to show that those sorts of structural connections really do exist and that they are not forced or artificial. Like the previous chapter, the goal now is not to show in any sort of comprehensive or definitive way how every part of Christian theology relates to the gospel, but more to point out some promising leads that would seem to confirm that general point. The second aim is to help anyone who thinks that Christian theology is beyond their capacity or their interest to see that it can be helpfully understood as just the extension of the gospel in different directions. That is, no Christian has to be an enthusiastic religious scholar or a student of theology in any formal sense in order to engage profitably with much of the fullness of Christian belief. All that is needed is an interest in the simple gospel message about Jesus and a willingness to continue down the paths that lead to more and more of its depth and implications. Third, the goal is to encourage anyone who loves to read and reflect on Christian theology to consider more of the links from the doctrine that they be might focusing on back to the core gospel message. Ultimately, the hope is that some will even think about whether there could be fruitful ways of mentally organising all of the different theological topics under the headings of the gospel, such that they are not only making links back from doctrines to gospel, but also seeing the gospel as the big framing idea that gives the overarching shape to all biblical truth.

To advance these goals, two approaches will be taken below: one looking at the gospel and systematic theology, which is what has mostly been discussed so far, and the other looking at the gospel and biblical theology, a discipline interested in things such as canonical theology, narrative theology or even metanarrative theology.

The gospel and systematic theology

Open almost any modern-day systematic theology textbook – the kind that offers an introductory overview of Christian doctrine and that is prescribed for undergraduate students in seminaries and theological colleges – and you will find pretty much the same set of topics laid out in broadly the same order. Generally speaking, after any preliminary materials, most of these volumes begin with a section on epistemology that covers topics such as revelation, authority and the Bible. Then comes the nature of God, often looking at his Trinitarian three-in-oneness as well as his attributes. Next will be a section on creation as made and intended by God, with humanity being the pinnacle of this. This is commonly followed by an examination of sin, its impacts and its consequences. Then comes Christology, outlining the person of Christ, and a section on his work and its accomplishments, which leads into a consideration of how people receive and benefit from Christ's atonement-making work. All of this can flow into a section on the Holy Spirit and, from here, ecclesiology follows, possibly with the inclusion of sacramental theology. Everything is then usually wrapped up with a closing part on eschatology. Of course, there are many, many variations on this simplified basic structure, with some textbooks treating different materials in a different order, some giving more or less space to the different matters and even having a somewhat different set of topics, and some using different language to map out their contents. Nonetheless, at a broad first pass, this is the arrangement of subjects that are usually considered to cover the body of historic, orthodox, Western Christian theology. And all of this is very much as it ought to be because these are the topics that the church and its great thinkers have recognised as the primary macro-matters about which the Bible is concerned, and therefore where they have given most of their attention over the centuries.

Looking over these major theological categories, we can once more note how the gospel obviously ties into the three that we have already been considering – Christology, atonement and eschatology – but we might then wonder how it relates to, say, epistemology, pneumatology or ecclesiology. As important and biblical as those subjects are, they do seem to be a step further removed from the central message of Jesus and not as obviously part of the gospel or its theology. But while the connections might not be quite as direct, they can still be legitimately made, and they have been considered to be natural and sensible over the history of Christian theologising.

A brief turn to the development of orthodox Christian doctrine through the centuries might be instructive at this point. We have plenty of good evidence showing that, from its earliest days, the church summarised its core beliefs in relatively standardised brief statements, versions of which we now call presentations of 'the rule of faith'.[2] Although not every instance of this Rule is identical with the rest, there is a great deal of commonality, and anyone who looks at the various articulations of the Rule will immediately recognise that they are very similar in form and content to the Apostles' Creed, which is ultimately just the crystallised and finalised form of the Rule. The relevance of this to systematic theology is primarily that the main topics of systematics can ultimately be understood as expansions of the statement of the Apostles' Creed. In its structure, the Creed recognises that God has revealed himself as Trinity (I believe in God, the Father almighty … I believe in Jesus Christ, his only Son, our Lord … I believe in the Holy Spirit …) and then it also affirms that he is Creator, that Christ is both divine and human, that Christ died and that there is a forgiveness of our sins, that Christ was resurrected and that there will be a general resurrection to eternal life, and that there is a holy and universal church founded by the apostles. Thus, in the Apostles' Creed, we have both the seeds and summaries of Christian thought on the nature of God, creation, sin, Christology, atonement, pneumatology, eschatology and ecclesiology – roughly the same spread of topics as found in today's systematic theology textbooks. For the present purposes, what is most important to add to this observation is the fact that the rule of faith and the Apostles' Creed do not only expand into full-blown Christian theology, but they also grow up out of the basic gospel message. Several scholars have shown this nicely, tracing the development of the proclamation of the basic Christian message into the rule of faith and thereby demonstrating how a more expanded expression of the gospel than the tight summary found in 1 Corinthians 15 ultimately touches on all of the major areas of doctrine.[3] And so, because the gospel develops into the Apostles' Creed and the Creed in turn expands into the various major areas of Christian doctrine, we see that the breadth of Christian theology is ultimately rooted in the gospel itself.[4] The historical connections exist, even if they are rarely highlighted.

There is at least one modern-day systematic theology textbook that explicitly grounds its presentation of the standard body of Christian belief in the gospel message: Michael Bird's *Evangelical Theology*.[5] The particular articulation of the gospel that Bird draws on is John Dickson's, which Bird summarises thus:

> The gospel is the announcement that God's kingdom has come in the life, death, and resurrection of Jesus of Nazareth, the Lord and Messiah, in fulfilment of Israel's Scriptures. The gospel evokes faith, repentance, and discipleship; its accompanying effects include salvation and the gift of the Holy Spirit.[6]

In line with 1 Corinthians 15, this summary includes the identity of Jesus as Messiah and both his life and his death. It also affects certain responses (faith and repentance), and has impacts (salvation) and manifestations (discipleship, spiritual gifting). This gospel pervades the doctrinal discussions throughout Bird's text as he regularly shows the connections between gospel and doctrine. And this is welcome, particularly as it gives eschatology a prominence that is proportional to the prominence of Jesus' resurrection in the gospel message, something not found in many other systematic theology volumes.[7]

Like all theology texts, there are many particular points in *Evangelical Theology* that might be disputed, but these do not invalidate the whole project of seeking to understand and cast the fuller body of Christian theology as being fundamentally connected to the core gospel message. While most systematic theology textbooks offer some kind of articulation of what their author believes is the primary theme of all theology, it would be welcome if more of them started with the gospel as Bird does. Given our present understanding of the gospel as the message of the death and resurrection of the Messiah, it could also be valuable to see one such book make an attempt to arrange all of the topics of systematics under the three major headings of Christology, atonement and eschatology, thereby reinforcing the gospel as the backbone for all of Christian belief. Contrary to being too forced or reductionistic, this would actually offer three wide bases from which all theology could be even-handedly developed, and the rationale for this structure would be strong, especially if the whole work opened with a fuller exploration and presentation of the gospel message itself. Perhaps in the Christology section, there could be not only considerations of Jesus as Second Person of the Trinity, but also of epistemology and even the material about the nature and attributes of the Father. After all, 'No one has ever seen God, but the one and only Son, who is himself God and is in the closest relationship with the Father, has made him known' (John 1:18). This means that right knowledge of God begins with Jesus. Likewise, the section on atonement might also incorporate pneumatology in recognition that one of the major and ongoing works of the Spirit is to apply the work of Christ personally in the lives of believers and those coming to faith today. And the part on eschatology could very naturally encompass creation and ecclesiology, coming to the former by way of the discussion on the new creation and the latter through consideration of the people of God as they will finally be constituted in the eternal church triumphant.

These ideas could be developed and expanded further, but it is enough for now to float the concept of shaping our systematic theology in this way. Of course, even without such a volume, there is likely to be both merit and utility in all Christians at least doing their own mental work to arrange their understandings of different doctrinal matters in gospel categories as one way of bringing a greater coherence to their own theological thought, and of ensuring that the gospel remains centred within it.

The gospel and biblical theology

Unlike systematic theology, there is no established agreement regarding either the meaning of the term 'biblical theology' or its content. The following quotation from the mid-1990s puts it nicely:

> Like apple pie, biblical theology is something most people find difficult to oppose (though there are always a few who dislike the taste); unlike apple pie, biblical theology is rather difficult to define … At one level, there cannot be a 'right' or 'wrong' definition of biblical theology. There is neither a stable, longstanding tradition of the use of the expression to which one might refer, nor an array of biblical passages that utilize the expression.[8]

Although more of a consensus has emerged in recent years, there is still enough variability in the use of term that we need to clarify how we are using it here.[9] There are several possibilities. For some, biblical theology simply means theology that is drawn from the Bible and which stands in contrast to, say, philosophical theology or even the theology of other religions. Taken this way, Christian biblical theology and systematic theology could be much the same thing, especially when there is a commitment to drawing all systematic theology from the Bible. However, this does not mean that a complete overlap between the terms and the disciplines therefore follows. Rather, it means that the difference between the two theologies would be in found in their methods and forms rather than in the truths that they maintain.

Others will distinguish biblical theology as theology which is *of* the Bible, not just taken *from* the Bible.[10] This sounds at first like a subtle difference, but it reflects a commitment to avoid beginning the work of theology by formulating external questions and then turning to the Bible for answers (for example, what does the Bible say about the how to vote, about God's relationship to time, or about technology?), or to prioritise synthetic categories that are then populated with biblical references (for example, omniscience, perichoresis or millennialism). Of course, there is nothing fundamentally wrong with either of these approaches to the Scriptures; they still result in a theology that is *from* the Bible. It is just that they are not the way that this understanding of biblical theology approaches its task. Rather, biblical theology that is *of* the Bible is more concerned with the theological truths that are plainly and straightforwardly expressed by the Bible itself, or by a given book or section of the Bible. This means that it is more concerned with questions such as, 'What is the theology of Paul's first Letter to the Thessalonians?' As it sought to answer that question, it would not be seeking to do so using categories like omniscience, perichoresis or millennialism, but might instead present its conclusions under the headings of faith, love and hope, which are more transparently the foci of that letter (1 Thessalonians 1:3, 5:8). Biblical theology thus conceived seeks to discover and present the theology of the Bible texts on their own terms. This means that finding the correct themes and categories is as much a part of the discipline as populating them.

For yet others, biblical theology can mean the teaching of the Bible considered in its literary and textual contexts. This is unlike systematic theology, which in its simplest (and sometimes least reliable) approach can take individual verses from the Bible as propositional data points without much interest in where those verses are found in their original biblical setting. So, for example, a systematic theologian might turn to Matthew 28:19 as a key text for proving the three-in-one nature of God, whose name is Father, Son and Holy Spirit, and they might place it alongside verses such as 2 Corinthians 13:14, where Paul's doxology supports the same conclusion. The biblical theologian, in contrast, would be more interested in the verse as a part of the closing section of Matthew's Gospel story, in which the risen Jesus gives his final Great Commission for his disciples to go and make disciples of all nations by baptising them in this name of God and teaching them to obey all of his commands (Matthew 28:19). The systematician working on the Trinity is less interested in the contextual setting and imperatives associated with the verse, while the biblical theologian wanting to understand the significance of the verse in its textual setting is less interested in its utility for building a case for the Trinity. Clearly, it is completely artificial to place these two theological enterprises into entirely different camps. The fact is that it is important to turn to different texts in different ways at different times for different purposes. We need a robust and standalone doctrine of the Trinity as much as we need to understand the theological flow of each part of Matthew's Gospel, and many readers are quite capable of engaging a biblical text in more than one way and can do so responsibly when necessary. The only point to make here is that this is another understanding of the task of biblical theology in contrast to that of its systematic cousin.

In thinking about biblical theology in this last way, we also see something of the change in the way that the task of Western theology has been undertaken historically. Following on from the church fathers of antiquity, by the Middle Ages, Christian theology had moved beyond considerations of the *sacra pagina* (sacred page), where theology was considered as the story of God read from the Bible, and on to reflections on *sacra doctrina* (sacred doctrine), where theological ideas were tackled more abstractly. The prime marker for this shift is the near-universal use that was made of Peter Lombard's *Four Books of Sentences* as the texts upon which most institutional study of theology was based in the West from the twelfth to the sixteenth century. Lombard gathered together all of the questions that had formerly arisen from reading through the Scriptures and categorised them so they were able to serve as the starting point for deeper theological explorations. But this meant that the starting point became synthetic doctrine rather than biblical texts read in their own contexts. This approach was continued through the period of high scholasticism, when great thinkers such as Thomas Aquinas worked through an extraordinarily detailed set of questions, sub-questions and sub-sub-questions in his magisterial *Summa Theologica*, which still stands as one of the most important contributions to Roman Catholic and scholastic theology. But so abstract and removed from the teaching of the Bible did many of these systematic questions seem to those outside the fold that the Roman Catholic theology was mocked by the Protestant reformers as an enterprise concerned with such pointless matters as how many angels could dance on the head of a pin! As part of their reaction to such wasteful and distracting pursuits, many of the sixteenth-century Protestants swung back in the other direction, a move captured well by Martin Luther's close companion Philip Melanchthon in the dedicatory letter at the opening of his *Loci Communes Theoligici*, which is recognised as the first summary theology text of the Reformation. There, he passionately says,

> There is no reason why we should labor so much on those exalted topics such as 'God,' 'The Unity and Trinity of God,' 'The Mystery of Creation,' and 'The manner of the Incarnation.' What, I ask you, did the Scholastics accomplish during the many ages they were examining only these points? Have they not, as Paul says, become vain in their disputations (Rom. 1:21), always trifling about universals, formalities, connotations, and various other foolish words? Their stupidity could be left unnoticed if those stupid discussions had not in the meantime covered up for us the gospel and the benefits of Christ … But as for the one who is ignorant of the other fundamentals, namely, 'The Power of Sin,' 'The Law,' and 'Grace,' I do not see how I can call him [*sic*] a Christian.[11]

Note that Melanchthon is not just proposing at alternative set of theological topics. More than that, he is claiming that, unlike the more broad and abstract headings such as 'God', 'Trinity', and 'Incarnation', his topics of 'Sin', 'Law', and 'Grace' are far more directly related to the main and explicit concerns of the Bible and are seen woven right through its unfolding storyline from start to finish. Indeed, this was the standard Protestant (and especially Lutheran) way of understanding the teaching of the Bible. It is a story of the relationship between God and his people that opened with the problem of sin, traced the people's struggles under the Old Testament law, and finally saw them resolved by the grace of God in Christ. This logical and somewhat chronological progression can be recognised as giving the standard shape not only to Melanchthon's own theology text, but also to Protestant theologies ever since, and it is the fruit of a kind of biblical-theological reading that produces its own categories and makes much of the logical flow of the Scriptures' teachings.

Yet another way to understand biblical theology is as the work of tracing a particular theme as it develops through the Bible. An example of this approach would be following the idea of the presence of God starting at Genesis 1 and 2, where God is directly involved with his creation and the people he has made in his image, right through to the end of the book of Revelation, where God dwells with his people in the new creation. On the way, many texts would need to be consulted to show both how the presence of God is manifested and experienced differently at different times, how that presence progressively changed over time from being veiled and indirect to being face to face and what God's presence meant or means at any particular point in history, including today. This yields potentially more dynamic information than a purely systematic approach, which might only consider the presence of God as a more static and universal idea that has been synthesised from all of the relevant texts without as much concern for the way that it changes over time or across a range of contextual settings.

Finally, biblical theology can be understood as the work of presenting a summary of the grand metanarrative of Scripture, usually emphasising one big theme, in a way that has some overlap with the highest-level work of systematic theologians. In this way of operating, biblical theology is about showing how the unfolding storyline of the Bible is all about salvation, love, freedom or perhaps some other concept, and then seeking to demonstrate how each part of the Bible feeds into that larger storyline or theme. This ties us back to those more narratival approaches to defining the gospel that we considered in chapter 1, where the goal was not only to show how the Bible is primarily concerned with a certain theme, but also to argue that that theme is at the heart of the gospel message itself. This is like quite a natural link to make. If the Bible is all about love from cover to cover, then there is good reason to suggest that the gospel is the message of love. If the Bible was all about sin, law and grace, as Melanchthon thought, then there is good reason to understand that these are central to the gospel, as he claims in the quotation above.

Without attempting to adjudicate between each of these conceptions of biblical theology, which can all be profitable and which are by no means mutually exclusive, we can at least suggest that it is helpful to our understanding of the pervasiveness of the gospel in the Bible to follow the last approach but in reverse. Rather than reading through the whole Bible, discerning a key theme, and concluding that it must be the gospel – the method of those who seek to define the gospel narratively – we can suggest that the gospel as defined by our work in 1 Corinthians 15 ought to be found relatively straightforwardly pervading the entire Bible. So, having located Christology, atonement and eschatology as the primary theological categories of the gospel – and potentially also as the major headings under which all other doctrine can be unfolded – it seems reasonable to suggest that using this approach, we should find these emphases laced throughout the Scriptures. If correct, this means that there will be no part of the Bible that does not ultimately intersect with some aspect of the message of the cross, the resurrection or the identity of Christ and thus some part of the heart of the gospel.

So, to continue the above example, when 1 Thessalonians addresses matters of faith, it is ultimately connecting with belief in the messiahship of Jesus and with a confidence in what has been achieved by his death and resurrection (1 Thessalonians 2:17–3:11). When Paul goes on to address love between believers, he discusses it with an underpinning of love for the same Messiah Jesus that flows into relationships with others (1 Thessalonians 3:12–4:12). And when he speaks of hope in this letter, it is plainly eschatological (1 Thessalonians 4:13–5:11). Approaching Paul's letter in this way, the particular theological undercurrents of 1 Thessalonians are thus preserved, but they are also openly related to the foundational truths of the gospel proper. Of course, this is a simple example, and considerably more work would be needed to make legitimate connections back to the gospel from every other part of Scripture without the entire exercise becoming forced and clumsy, just as more work would be needed to account for all of the nuances of 1 Thessalonians. Nonetheless, if the general approach is legitimate, then similar connections between text and gospel could be sought every time the Bible is studied. Wherever we look, we should find something related to atonement, eschatology or Christology, in the full expanse of their meanings, and then see the links back to the death, resurrection or identity of Jesus. Obviously, this could prove to be incredibly fruitful for presenting the gospel from any part of the Bible and for deepening the biblical knowledge of believers without ever moving them away from the gospel.

Gospel theology

Bringing together the relationships between the gospel and systematic theology, and the gospel and biblical theology is not at all novel. While there are of course many Bible readers who might not automatically make all of these associations, there are also many who do and who do so in a range of different ways. However, as much as the latter group is to be commended for their integrated approach to the Bible, there are perhaps some who make the connections too tenuously and formulaically. This is seen within some evangelical circles with the common conclusion that Christ's sacrificial death for sinners is the true focal point of many texts, even those where atonement is nowhere clearly on view. Perhaps broadening out to see the gospel as the basis and culmination of eschatology and Christology as well as atonement could help to prevent such routine and sometimes unconvincing interpretations, even as we must acknowledge that doing so would not automatically shut down other simplistic analyses of different texts. Even so, this could be a step forward in more accurately identifying and highlighting the real gospel threads of different parts of the Bible, and it could be welcomed as an approach by those who recognise the centrality of the gospel to every part of Christian life and who hold the evangelical commitment to a high view of all Scripture.

At this juncture, I suggest that there could be some significant value in adopting the idea of 'gospel theology' as a supplement to both systematic and biblical theology.[12] The term would not represent a discipline altogether separate from the other theologies, but it would rather capture the approach to each as discussed above. That is, by the term 'gospel theology', we would indicate the particular framing of systematics around the three theological pillars of the gospel and also the practice of identifying those pillars as they undergird each part of the entire canon of Scripture. This could prove of use to those wanting language for the project of thinking through the connections between any given doctrine that they are studying and the gospel proper, and to those wanting to read through and understand different parts of the Bible in their own literary contexts while at the same time wanting to keep sharply aware of the pervasiveness of gospel themes. In both cases, there could be some great, tangible benefits for practical ministry that are worth thinking through.

This need for theology to be expressed in works of ministry and for works of ministry to be grounded in good theology is what we will start to explore in our final full chapter. However, before doing that, we must first give a little space to thinking about the gospel and one particular topic of theology: hamartiology, the theology of sin.

8

The whole gospel meets the whole problem of sin

One topic of theology requires some special attention given its particular relation to the gospel, its general importance in any scheme of Christian doctrine and that fact that it is very often conceived of too narrowly. That topic is sin. In the rawness of its impacts, the reality of sin is well known to anyone who has spent any time in pastoral ministry, just as it is to anyone who spends time in close relationships with other people and to anyone who has taken pause to reflect honestly on their own life.

In the academy, much attention goes to the complex issue of the source of sin and its propagation through the human race – matters formally addressed by the Augustinian-Calvinistic (or otherwise approached) doctrines of original sin, which can be outlined straightforwardly enough, but which do not always satisfactorily resolve every important and relevant exegetical question about the key texts and which can require some quite complex argumentations.[1] Of course, when it comes to evangelical articulations of the gospel message, sin usually has a prominent place, although it is too often presented one-dimensionally.

Without wanting to caricature, it is relatively standard to hear gospel presentations that begin by setting up the ubiquitous problem of human sinfulness and the divine judgement that all humans therefore deserve. This then moves to a discussion about humanity's complete inability to restore itself to God's favour, but then also the good news that Christ has borne the penalty for sins in his death, which means that all that remains necessary is for individuals to turn to him, trusting in the effectiveness of what he has already done. So frequent are evangelistic messages with this shape that they almost seem to be built from a common template that only requires the insertion of the scriptural text of the day and some personal illustrations in order to produce the finished script. On a bigger scale, there are churches and even whole denominations that deliberately shape all of their patterns of public worship around this single dynamic of sin and atonement for it, week in week out, reminding the congregation of their sinful nature and offering a corporate confession of sin before turning to thanksgiving for the forgiveness found in Christ.

The roots of these formulae can be traced back to the Protestant Reformation of the sixteenth century, when the question of personal faith and salvation came to the fore over against the priorities of the old Roman Catholic rhythms of public worship. As just one example, the Church of England of the time reshaped all of its sanctioned corporate worship services around the ideas that human beings are sinners in need of salvation, and that salvation comes through Christ alone. This resulted in its entire volume of official outlines for liturgical services, the *Book of Common Prayer*, having very little deviation from this macro theme.[2] To be sure, even as many people are drawn to the formal services of some parts of the Church of England or its daughter Anglican and Episcopalian churches due to their considerable biblical depth and artistic beauty, it is understandable that many also find them stiflingly rigid not only in form, but also in content.

While there might be fair reasons to call for these types of communications to be freshened up for different audiences and contexts, our understanding of the gospel would confirm that they do get right to its core. Atonement flows from the heart of the gospel. Therefore, no case ought to be made for changing the truths that are being shared in these ways, even if the means of doing so could be given some more creative attention. But as should also be clear from everything that we have outlined so far in this book, an argument can and should be made that these types of gospel presentations do not do justice to the *whole* gospel. They do not adequately relay the truths of both the death and resurrection of Jesus, who was and is the unique God-man. In their way of focusing in on the problem of sin, they have impressively showcased one part of the gospel message while potentially eclipsing the others. Perhaps they do this because they are consciously working out of an atonement-centric understanding of the gospel, akin to some of those that we considered in chapter 1. Perhaps they are committed to unashamedly owning and championing the theological heritage of the Reformation, which has been faithfully preserved and passed down by Protestant churches over the centuries. Perhaps they are mimicking the witness of the New Testament, in which gospel proclamation often emphasises just one part of the message. This is something that we will return to in the next chapter when considering some of the ways that the whole gospel can shape practical ministry. Although some of these reasons are highly commendable, it does not immediately follow that the atoning death of Christ to pay the price for human guilt is the *only* part of the gospel that *ever* needs to be presented. It will surely be appropriate and helpful to bring the other aspects of the gospel to the fore sometimes, at the very least to safeguard against communicating that the message is narrower than it really is.

One predicted response to this concern might be to de-emphasise sin in some gospel presentations, or at least to avoid always starting with the problem of sin. Sadly, some churches and some individual Christians take this too far. While their motives here might be good on one level – they are seeking to foreground the more attractive parts of the Christian faith rather than those that are potentially off-putting – this move might also reflect a thin theology of sin, as though it leads to nothing more than guilt, judgement and condemnation. Certainly, these connections cannot be severed, but there is also more to be said about sin and the ways that it is met by the gospel. Like the gospel, sin too is multidimensional, which does not mean that our recognition of human guilt and culpability needs to be diluted, but rather that these are further compounded by additional issues that are the terrible expression of sin in the world.

At the risk of just being too neat and tidy, or even of potentially forcing a fit to a model, it seems that sin can be well-understood as having three major aspects, each of which is met by one of the three different parts of the gospel message. First, as just affirmed, sin does lead to guilt and culpability for the sinner. Sinners are rightly held accountable for their wrongdoings by a just and completely pure God. And it is true that the only remedy to this is the forgiveness that comes exclusively through sin's price being paid by Christ on behalf of sinners who accept this gift of unmerited grace. Again, this is the somewhat standard evangelical interaction with the doctrine and reality of sin, and it is one that ought to be maintained.

Second, we can add that, in a fallen world, sin leads to real suffering that is not always associated with any godly guilt directly resulting from any particular actions of those who suffer. Take, for example, a situation where a person at a market has their phone snatched away by an opportunistic thief, or perhaps one where a sober driver is seriously injured in a car accident caused by a drunk driver, or even the horrendous reality of civilians wounded by the military assaults of another nation that had invaded their own. In these cases, the shopper, the sober driver and the civilians must be understood as victims who suffer because of sin, not as those who in these settings are guilty of sin. They therefore do not need to be called to repentance at this point, and the message of Christ dying for their sins, while unchangingly true, is not the right one for the moment. But the gospel in its fullness is for every moment, and when people are innocently suffering it offers the hope that ultimately finds its true anchor in Christ's resurrection and the eschatology that flows from it, rather than from his cross and atonement. Someone suffering because of the sin of theft might need to be given hope for an afterlife where thieves do not steal any more than moths and vermin destroy (Matthew 6:19). Another who is sick or injured might need to hear of the certainty of bodily restoration and the subsequent imperishability that will be part of the general resurrection of all believers from the dead (1 Corinthians 15:50–54). Another who has been mistreated in war might need to know about the final justice that will be meted out on the last day for every evil deed committed and every word spoken, as well as the eternal peace and security that will be established at Christ's return.[3] Essentially, some will need to know that the sins they have been victim to and the suffering that has resulted are all addressed by the truths connected to the resurrection of Jesus. This is a gospel message, even if it is not about the cross and the forgiveness of the person hearing it. Sin has an impact on more than our righteous and moral standing before God, and while the gospel does bring about our forgiveness, it brings more than just our forgiveness.

Third, we must also recognise that the New Testament speaks of sin as slavery (John 8:34; Romans 6:16–18). This is related to the way that sin results in suffering because slavery is a cause of great suffering and is again not usually something for which we can present an obvious cause-and-effect explanation where the cause is the enslaved person's own wrongdoing. But in addition to this, slavery also holds people against their will in a lasting detrimental situation. To be a slave is to be deprived of liberty, to be forced to be somewhere that you do not want to be, to have to do or endure things against your will, and for which you do not receive a fair reward. Slavery also means not having any obvious or preferred way out.[4] This was very much the reality for the Israelites in the opening of the book of Exodus when they were enslaved in Egypt. Their history of being in that captivity and then being freed by God became a central part of the founding narrative that established their national identity (Exodus 1–12). We cannot understand the Israelites or God's saving work among them without understanding that they were trapped in and then freed from the sinful state of enslavement.

The New Testament says that bondage to sin is a captivity in some ways similar to this, and from its perspective it is easy to look back on the Old Testament and see that slavery to sin had always been a bigger problem for Israel than even their physical captivity.[5] We see this in the fact that even after God had used Moses to free his people from their slavery, they were still bound by their own sinful natures and so regularly dishonoured and disobeyed God, thus repeatedly bringing upon themselves his righteous judgement (for example, Exodus 16:1–3, 32:1–35; Numbers 14:1–45). They turned out to be more enslaved to sin than they were to Pharaoh. This leads to the other aspect of sin as slavery: it is not only related to suffering, but also to guilt, as it is not a captivity imposed by someone 'out there' but a captivity to our own worst, fallen selves. To be enslaved to sin is to be trapped in a pattern of wrongdoing that attracts God's judgement. The blame cannot all be shifted to someone else or to external circumstances, and yet at the same time there is no way to take charge and break free of the bondage either. Clearly, this is not a place where anyone who understands what is going on would want to be. The gospel addresses the situation of being enslaved to sin partly through the cross of Christ (forgiveness is found there even for recurring sins) and through his resurrection (there is a future hope of being remade as a fully Spirit-led person who always and only seeks and does right things). But even as the cross erases the past, it does not automatically prevent the sinner from reoffending. And even as the resurrection ensures a pure future, that is still to come and so cannot be experienced in its fullness now. Yet the gospel has more to give through the identity of Jesus as divine Messiah and Lord, although the unexpected twist in this is that true freedom from sin is only found through being enslaved to Jesus as our master.

We learn from the New Testament, and from reflection on common experience, that human beings always give themselves to the service of someone or something. It turns out that being enslaved is in fact an inescapable part of human nature (cf. 2 Peter 2:19b). If people are not enslaved to someone else, then they will be enslaved to themselves, to an ideology, to a purpose, to an aspiration, to something. Everyone is controlled by something. Of course, the problem is that being primarily dedicated to and directed by anyone or anything apart from the true God will ultimately prove to be bad for us and it is, almost by definition, sin. A person whose first commitment is not to God has displaced God from the highest place in their mind and life and replaced him with someone or something else. This is wrong even for good things that are rightly important to most people – things such as family, justice or peace – if these become more important than Jesus. Of course, God is also committed to such good things and wants his people to pursue the best versions of them passionately, but this requires their motivations and perspectives to be set correctly.

It is very possible, and indeed very right, to serve family, justice, peace and other good things precisely as an outworking of our fidelity to God. But committing to exactly the same things only because they matter most to us personally is sinful to the degree that it is the working out of our own priorities rather than his. Outwardly, the actions can be the same, but what is driving from the inside is very different. And again, this way of operating does not just incur guilt; it is enslaving, as people whose first commitment is not to God become bound by the range of obligations, requirements and demands of someone or something else, which cannot be left behind without transferring to serve the obligations, requirements and demands of an alternative. It is impossible to live without serving someone or something.

To make slavery to anything other than God more foolish still, the truth is that the greatest outcomes for even the good things we might seek after can only be realised in and through God anyway. All else being equal, no matter how good a family is, it will be better when served by someone motivated by dedication to God. No matter how much justice can be achieved, a greater and purer justice will be achieved by those seeking it in line with God's priorities. No matter what peace is settled, a deeper peace will arrive if brought by those who bring it in the name of God. This is because God is the ultimate source of all that is good and right and pure and worthy, and so anything that is achieved with the goal of bringing glory and honour to him, and with particular attention to his ways of achieving it, will be more in line with what is best for everyone and everything. Slavery to anything other than Christ not only results in people acting against God's will, but it also leads to lesser final outcomes for whoever or whatever is served, even when they are good things.

In contrast to all of this, the Bible teaches that the way to be truly free is to become a slave of Christ. Christ's slaves are freed from all of the evil, sin and burdens that tie people down and that lie behind their spiritually destructive habits. Given that he is the highest truth and the greatest good, being closely bound to Jesus and living according to his will and direction is the best, healthiest and holiest way to live and the fullest way to bless others. In belonging to him, there is freedom from the selfishness of living for self, freedom from the stresses of always needing to get everything right, freedom from the anxiety of uncertain outcomes, freedom from striving to meet life's unending needs and of course freedom from the consequences of living at odds with the only source of life. Living as a dedicated follower of Jesus means freedom from everything that is ultimately bad for us, even as there will still be very real suffering, struggles and challenges to live through while we wait for eternity. And eternity must always be kept in view. To think that having full allegiance to Jesus would free a person from everything that hurts and binds them in this life would be a form of prosperity gospel, where the highest good can be taken as being material, physical and temporal. Externally imposed slaveries might still be the reality for many followers of Jesus, just as some of the slaveries of a person's own making can remain hard to escape from – for example, addictions to things including to illicit drugs and alcohol.[6] But the central freedoms of Christ are freedoms from the guilt of sin and its penal consequences, from the impossible task of winning God's favour and from the fears and futility that are the result of not belonging to God.

Despite the rendering in some English versions of the Bible, the Apostle Paul introduces himself in several of his letters as a 'slave' of Jesus, rather than a 'servant'.[7] The latter sounds more like a position that earns a wage and comes with days off and workplace regulations, whereas the former more appropriately captures the idea of total and absolute submission without bargaining power. Paul did not come to be a servant of Jesus through some negotiated agreement, and he did not feel that he could resign and look elsewhere for a better post. Rather, he understood himself as being bought by Christ, who therefore came to own and rule him outright.

This idea of being unwaveringly submissive to God is also implied in the very identification of Jesus as God's long-awaited and ultimate Messiah or king of both the Jewish people and humanity at large. Serving this king as a faithful subject of his kingdom is one way to think about being a person who acknowledges the royal identity of Christ as captured in the gospel. But another way to understand the same reality is to see oneself as being joyfully enslaved to Jesus, having been freed from slavery to sin and the law and transferred over to his complete custody, care and control. Yes, this can sound at first like a loss of freedom in the way that freedom is commonly understood in Western culture – the choice and opportunity to do whatever we want and especially whatever serves our own interests and desires – but as we have already seen, it really implies a transfer from possession by things that are ultimately destructive into the belonging of the one who loves us the most and who is able to fill us in ways that no one and nothing else can. This of course lines up with our own deepest desires anyway, and when we see that, we realise that it is exactly what we want.

We have seen that some evangelicals take the gospel as being the message that Jesus is Lord, the King of God's kingdom, the rightful ruler of everyone and everything. They remind us that the supreme leader of all was never Caesar or Herod, nor is it any leader or figurehead in today's world, and as created beings, we are certainly not our own rightful masters.[8] The biblical conception is that Jesus is the supreme leader of all, and the acknowledgement of and commitment to this truth is needed for someone to be a Christian. The converse side of this point is that not submitting to the lordship of Jesus necessarily means following the call of someone or something else. In some cases, this is thought of positively – for example, in Western culture's dedication to financial independence and unrestricted sexual expression. Of course, in other cases, it is recognised as being a terrible thing, like when someone cannot break free from an addiction to opioids or violent online pornography. But whether seen in a good or poor light by humanity, the teaching of the Scriptures is that it is sinful to have anyone or anything apart from God as a first priority. For this, the gospel solution – worked inside us by the power of the Holy Spirit – is not just to turn to Christ's cross and repent for past wrongdoing (although that will be necessary), and not only to look to the resurrection for future freedom (although that will be a great blessing), but also to give our allegiance to Jesus the Messiah, to put him in first place.[9] The only way to be released from the enslaving power of sin is to become fully bound to Christ, whose slaves are freed from all of sin's tyrannies and its destructive ends. The third theological pillar of the gospel, the identity of King Jesus the God-man, addresses enslavement, which is the third expression of sin that we encounter all too regularly in our fallen world.[10]

There is nothing neat about sin, or pastoral theology

While dividing up the different aspects of sin is helpful for understanding its nature and impacts in some more detail, the lived reality is never quite so neat. People can bear culpability and be victims and be trapped all at the same time. The above-mentioned shopper who is robbed at the market might have been lavishly and selfishly spending ill-gotten money in a community of very poor people whom they had exploited for years. The drunk driver might have become addicted to alcohol after being exposed to it by abusive parents as a small child. The invading nation might have been dangerously threatened by a hostile local government that the wounded civilian vocally supported. Although these are fictitious examples, life can be very much like this. Another informative and less imaginary example is that of the illegal drug addict. It would be possible to see them as a guilty criminal because of their willing purchase and use of substances that are strictly outlawed and because of their lawless behaviours while high. Or they might be understood as a suffering victim, someone whose life is in all kinds of terrible mess because of the impact of a dangerous substance, the pressures put on them by those dealing or even the social context that took them away from so many alternative options and opportunities. Or they might be recognised as a slave, who has no remaining willpower to resist the physiological and psychological pull of the drugs that they have become dependent on or to break out of the damaging patterns of life and behaviour that they find themselves in. Each of these evaluations might lead to different conclusions about the appropriate consequences and the ways to avoid them. The offender ought to be judged, but they could potentially discharge their debt to society or even be pardoned. The sufferer needs medical and community care and a change of context to have their living pains eased. The slave needs a recovery programme or clinical and therapeutic interventions to break their bad habits. But chances are that the addict is guilty and suffering and enslaved all at the same time, meaning that a multifaceted approach will be needed to interact with them holistically. So too with many sins.

A one-dimensional analysis might be of some help, but it can still leave considerable parts of the problem unaddressed. A mature Christian diagnosis of any sin will need to evaluate it across its whole range of causes and impacts, and this can require a great deal of pastoral wisdom and discernment. It will not always help if the very first move in ministering the gospel to a suffering victim is to call them to repentance, or an addict to hope in a potentially very distant future, or a guilty person to the freedom of Christ. To be sure, every aspect of the gospel is important for all people, and over time everyone will need to grow in their comprehension of all of them. But this does not mean that every part of the gospel speaks as directly to every person's immediate, most pressing needs. This is important to understand because misapplication of the gospel can actually undermine the gospel in at least two ways. First, any time a problem is misdiagnosed and a wrong remedy subsequently offered, the results are likely to be poor. A simple analogy would be going to a doctor with a broken leg and being prescribed an ointment for an ear infection. Either the problem or the solution (or both) has been misunderstood, the result is that the leg will not be healed and the inappropriate application of the unnecessary ointment might even do damage. Second, though, is the fact that such mistakes can dilute people's confidence in both the person they have turned to for help and the solutions they propose. No one would return to the medical professional who had failed them so badly, nor would they recommend them to anyone else. Similarly, if the gospel is misapplied, both it and the person speaking it can lose credibility. Telling a survivor of a serious accident caused by a drunk driver that the first thing they need to do is repent is unlikely to be effective either at getting them to confess any relevant sins in that moment or giving them hope for a better future, and it is unlikely to make them excited about commending that gospel to others. Even when we understand sin as being the root cause of all of the world's problems and the gospel as being the ultimate solution, it is necessary to find the right connection between the multidimensional cause and the multidimensional remedy. Good theology is always applied with close attentiveness to pastoral contexts.

A third way in gospel theology

Thinking about the multifaceted nature of sin, and leaving pastoral considerations aside for the moment, we see another way in which the gospel helps us to understand, organise and interact with other topics of Christian theology. This might even be a third approach to gospel theology alongside its use in relation to systematic theology and biblical theology as discussed in the previous chapter. To recap what was said regarding those two theologies, we found that bringing the theological shape of the gospel to the major categories of Christian doctrine can give a structure within which all synthetic beliefs can be organised, and having the major doctrines of the gospel in mind when reading through the Bible contextually can help us to map a good path from any part of the Scriptures to the good news of Jesus. But in considering sin, we have been looking at one particular doctrine and seeing the different ways that it connects to each of the different aspects of the theology of the gospel. If systematic theology involves setting doctrines within a wider theological grid, and biblical theology lets us see the gospel shot through the whole Bible, this third approach lets us see more of the full gospel connections that might exist within a given doctrine. This would aid us in further thickening up our understanding of that doctrine, as well as better integrating it with our overarching gospel framework. Two more basic examples of how this might work might be helpful.

First, ecclesiology. Coming to the doctrines of the church through the lens of the gospel directly and easily articulates with our understanding of the church as the body of Christ: his identity gives the church its identity. This means that Jesus' people in community ought to be sacrificial as he was, ought to live with eternal values in anticipation of their eternal state as he did and ought represent God to the world just as he imaged the Father to us. But the gospel also shows us how the church must understand itself as a forgiven people who live by the cross, a community who never presume any special standing with God due to their own merit and who never exclude others because of their perceived lack of merit. Rather, the humble thankfulness of sinners who have been forgiven through the death of Jesus should be characteristic of the church and the interactions of its members. Additionally, the church should be a people of joyful hope, ever looking to the resurrection of Jesus for the strength and certainty required to persevere through whatever trials it might face until it is gathered around him in its final, triumphant state. The identity of Christ, his cross and his resurrection are all powerful within our thinking about the doctrine of the church.

Second, pneumatology. The gospel grid helps us to see that a primary work of the Spirit is to open our eyes to Jesus as the divine-human Messiah, to go beyond just reading or hearing about his teaching and miracles to being convicted of his identity because of them and then honouring him for who he is. Indeed, we cannot know Jesus rightly apart from his Spirit working in us, which, as we have seen, would seem to be the reason he said that it was actually to his people's advantage that he departed from earth and returned to heaven.[11] Only then would the Advocate, the Spirit, come (John 16:7). But following on, we recognise that the Spirit also helps each of us to see our own need for Jesus' death and then gives us hearts to turn to him in faith and repentance. At the same time, when we wonder why some people do not come to faith despite having heard the message of forgiveness in Jesus clearly and repeatedly, we can recognise this as the free working of the Spirit and not only as a failure of our evangelistic methods (although we ought to be open to thinking a lot about our evangelistic methods too). And as the Holy Spirit is the one who not only helps us to acknowledge from our hearts who Jesus is and respond to what he has done for us on his cross, he then also transforms us into the new creation people we are meant to be growing into as we anticipate our participation in the eternal future life as people resurrected like Jesus. By the Spirit, we lead spiritual lives, holy lives, which are really resurrection lives. Our pneumatology intersects with all of our resurrection theology, as it does with our atonement theology and our Christology.

Clearly, there is much more to be said in any fully developed theologies of sin, the church and the Spirit than there is room for here. But what we have done in considering each of these through the lens of the theology of the gospel has demonstrated how they can be meaningfully filled out by the gospel and tied back to the gospel. Reciprocally, these kinds of explorations also enable us to see some more of the fullness and reach of the theology of the gospel too.

9

The gospel and practical ministry

Exploring and unpacking the gospel is an exercise in sharpening and deepening the theological foundations of the Christian faith. As such, it is an intrinsically important exercise for every Christian who is able to do it. At their starkest, the results of neglecting such an important task could be a thin, partial, imbalanced or even outright mistaken understanding of the core of God's work and revelation. Even so, the Christian faith has never been just about the comprehension of and assent to a set of important truths. While it is true that what we do does not make us right with God, it is nonetheless impossible to escape the fact that God calls people to live actively in line with their biblically informed convictions. Christianity is both a mind-shaping and life-shaping religion, with the shaping of the mind critical to the necessary shaping of the life. This being so, we must close off our study of the gospel by asking what we are meant to do with what we have learned. How is the message of the death and resurrection of the Messiah meant to direct our lives of obedient service at a practical level?

There are innumerable good answers to this question and, as with the last few chapters, our purpose now is not to be comprehensive, but only to give some examples of the sorts of connections that we might make between the gospel, gospel theology and praxis. It would also be well worth us spending some solid time working out how the gospel ought to give shape to our emotions, attitudes, dispositions, relationships, aspirations, sorrows, fears, characters, devotions, prayers and so, so much more, but these are matters to be tackled in other places. For the present, the goal is far more functional and directed towards active Christian ministry and, in particular, ministries of the word (even as we recognise that the distinction made between word- and non-word-ministries is often too sharp). In this, we must be clear that we definitely do not think that these word ministries are only carried out by vocational or 'professional' Christians, as though those who are paid to work in Christian settings are the only ones with the privilege or responsibility of opening up the Bible with others or the only ones who need to relate the gospel to their services. The step towards some kind of word ministry is one that all Christians with capacity should take, whatever their context or particular opportunities.

The examples below are somewhat artificially categorised and far neater than will be found in the real world, but hopefully they give a good lead into further thinking about living out the gospel in lives of faithful and active service. For simplicity, we will think of two broad contexts: proclaiming the gospel to those who are not believers and growing existing followers of Jesus in their understanding and embrace of the gospel and of gospel-shaped living.

Proclaiming the gospel

Often, opportunities to share the gospel come up organically in our conversations as we share our lives with friends, neighbours, colleagues and the other people whom we come across in our day-to-day activities. There are also times when we deliberately plan towards a particular moment to share the gospel with someone, perhaps drawing on a specific Bible passage before lovingly encouraging them towards a response of repentance and faith. This is the sort of thing that happens in some churches at regular evangelistic, outreach or seeker services, but it can also happen at other special one-off events, short courses for small groups and even in our one-to-one personal conversations. In any of these sorts of settings, the approach is often to begin with a chosen passage of Scripture – one that is explicitly about a particular aspect of the gospel or where the connections to the message of Jesus are quick and easy to make – and to demonstrate its relevance to those in attendance. While all of this is commendable, it is unfortunately too often true that this approach to evangelism tends to circle back to the same limited selection of texts, or back to just one aspect of the theology of the gospel.

One problem with repeatedly explaining the gospel from only a small number of texts is that it can send the signal that the core Christian message is either absent from, or at least opaque in, most of the rest of the Bible. It can also teach people the bad habit of studying passages of the Bible completely out of the literary and canonical contexts of which they are a part and in which God deliberately caused them to be preserved. And then the problem with only ever teaching a single part of the theology of the gospel is that it can signal that the central body of Christian truth is narrower than it really is. Perhaps the showcase example of this is when a preacher follows up their great atonement-centred Good Friday sermon with another atonement-centred sermon on Easter Sunday instead of with a message explaining anything of the biblical eschatology that flows from Jesus' resurrection. From this, the visitor to the Easter church services certainly hears an essential truth, but they only learn one part of the fuller gospel message. In addition, these repetitive approaches to gospel proclamation can prove to be quite ineffective if they always fail to meet the felt needs of the people who are listening.

Effective communication is never simply about one person handing over a package of information to another. Hugh Mackay has called this the 'injection myth' to capture the false belief that a message will be automatically and irresistibly absorbed by any person who hears it irrespective of how they feel about either the message itself or the person sharing it. This would be to assume that the message was like a medicine injected into the body, which will take its effect irrespective of how the patient feels about either it or the health professional administering it.[1] A better analogy for the effective communication of a message might be a fielder catching a fast-moving cricket ball that has been hit in their general direction. The catcher needs not only to be present, but also to be ready and willing in the precise moment, and they need to have been more generally well-prepared to take this kind of catch before they even walk out onto the pitch for this particular match. That is, the fielder's readiness plays a huge part in whether or not the ball will be caught, just as the listener's readiness plays a major part in whether or not they will accept a speaker's message.

Of course, unlike the batter in cricket, the evangelist is very much hoping that what they send in their listener's direction will be easily grasped and held onto, and this means that it is often important for the person sharing the gospel not only to speak the message, but also to do whatever they can to make it as easy as possible for their hearers to receive it. This is where being attentive to people's felt needs is vitally important. While it might ultimately be the case that a Christian who is sharing the gospel can be quite correct about every person's ultimate needs for forgiveness, hope and identity in Christ, this does not mean that any gospel message they speak will automatically connect with a person who is not feeling those needs at that moment. Not everyone will be ready to receive it. Another example might help to make the point here. Imagine a person who is open enough to hearing the Christian message, but who is not at all burdened by guilt and who, relatively speaking, lives a pretty decent life. They respect other people, they do not break the law, they are generous, hospitable and charitable, and they have not had any major relationship breakdowns. To be met with a gospel message that tells them that they are totally depraved, living in a state of sin and in need of salvation might be true to the teaching of the Bible, but it might not connect with anything much that this person is feeling, or has ever felt, about themselves. As a consequence, they might find it hard to internalise the message of their guilt in a hurry, and they might be unconvinced of their need to rush to Jesus' cross for the solution to the problem that they had never come to feel that they had. It might be that a more effective evangelistic approach for this person is speaking to them about the resurrection's message of hope, or about the identity of Jesus as true Lord of all. Of course, the only way to really know what is most likely to connect with someone is by knowing them personally. The better we know our audience's felt needs, the more we will have a sense of which part of the gospel will meet them.

It is well worth recognising that in the New Testament, the records of evangelisation often emphasise just one or two parts of the message of Jesus and not necessarily every part of the gospel all at once. Paul can know 'nothing … except Jesus Christ and him crucified' when with the Corinthians (1 Corinthians 2:2) and yet focus on the resurrection when debating in Athens (Acts 17:22–31), while Peter presses the identity of Jesus at Pentecost (Acts 2:14–41). In no case can we imagine that the apostles ultimately planned to leave their audience with only a truncated gospel message and never to move on to the other aspects of the gospel.

Rather, it makes far more sense to understand them as simply having different starting points for communicating the gospel with different people in different situations and therefore with different felt needs. This is actually a very important point for gospel teaching generally. While it is good to recognise that there are different facets to the gospel and different theologies that flow from each, it is not the case that every part of the gospel needs to be shared in every communication of it. That is, we must recognise that there is nothing illegitimate about speaking to just one part of the gospel at any time, conscious that more will need to be added later. Evangelism does not need to cover everything all at once; it can quite properly zero in on one aspect of the gospel at a given moment, discerning that it is the right aspect for the occasion, and that there might be more suitable times to go into the rest.

Following this thinking, it is powerful for us to draw on the fullness of the gospel in evangelism and to consider whether there are different aspects of the gospel that might have more direct resonances with certain people at different times. Excitingly, this means that we might be able to present the gospel more effectively in a wider range of settings than we would if we held onto the idea that evangelism can only draw on a limited range of texts or on just one part of the theology of the gospel. Perhaps for some, it is not the need for atonement that is most acutely felt in the first instance, but the need for hope or the freedom and peace of secure belonging. If so, sharing the good news of the resurrection or the identity of Jesus might make a quicker connection with them. One of these aspects of the gospel might meet our listeners closer to where they are and find them more likely to be receptive to what we would love them to know. Again, it is clear that to do this well will involve knowing something about the people with whom we are communicating, having some sense of what is going on for them and perhaps even knowing this beyond what is obvious from casual social interactions. In some cases, people's felt needs are easy to identify, but in others, they will only be revealed through the course of more extended interactions and relationships. Everyone hoping to share the gospel must recognise that evangelism often requires this kind of invested concern for individuals' lives because, despite so many of the truly great efforts of our rational apologists, the reality is that most people do not first believe facts; they first believe other people. The people they believe are those they trust, and those they trust are those who have a genuine interest in them. There is wisdom in the notion that we need to love people into the kingdom as much as argue them in.

With all of this in mind, below are three simplified examples of what sharing the gospel with non-Christians could look like. These account for their different circumstances, connect to different parts of the gospel message and draw from different New Testament passages. We will not go into any detailed exegetical work here; we will simply just sketch what this type of witnessing could look like.

Publicly proclaiming Jesus' forgiveness

Picture this scene: in an evangelistic presentation to an audience of several hundred, the speaker draws from Mark 7:1–23 to explain that people's actions and concerns can sometimes appear to be noble and upright, yet they actually arise from negative feelings or intentions. She explains that in the Christian understanding, the real moral issue is around what is going on deep inside our hearts, and what we see on the surface can only be properly assessed as an overflow of what is inside. Given this framing, she asks her listeners whether they know that, deep down inside themselves, there are some ugly truths that they are pretty sure would not be well-received by decent folks, let alone a God who is all purity, and whether they have a secret longing for cleansing and acceptance for all of the hidden, dark things they carry within. She then goes on to present the good news that while those worst parts of ourselves should indeed ultimately lead to our rejection by God, God has instead done something radical. He has not ignored our worst selves, as though our inner state does not really matter all that much to him, but has instead placed the natural consequences for them on his Son, Jesus. The central reason that Jesus died was because he was taking all of our deserved judgement in our place. And the reason he did this was because he loves us, just like his heavenly Father loves us, and neither of them want to be separated from us. Even our hidden motivations, desires and inner thoughts – all those things that no one else might ever see but that we know are there – have all been accounted for in Jesus' death and so no longer need to stand between us and God. Full forgiveness is found in Christ.

Sharing hope for the hopeless

A man is meeting with a group of older teenagers who have all had some pretty rough experiences and emotional challenges and who are all feeling relatively bleak about their lives and futures. Collectively, they're looking for love, acceptance and hope, but they cannot realistically see much changing for them. The leader reads from 1 Peter 1:3–9 and talks about the incredible riches of God's promises and how wonderful they are, but he also shows that they are promises for eternity and will not necessarily be experienced before then. He shows that the text acknowledges that some people whom God loves very much might well suffer through various trials in this life, making plain that the Bible is honest and not naive about this. God gets what is going on. One of the group members scoffs and suggests that this is just religious wishful thinking – nice words that can never be proven and that make God sound loving, even though the reality is that he leaves people in terrible situations. The leader agrees that this is certainly how it feels a lot of the time. But he goes on to say that in the Christian understanding, Jesus' resurrection is what changes that. If Jesus really rose from the dead, then he shows that there really is a life beyond this one, and he also shows that it is a glorious and transformed life that leads on to heaven. The risen Jesus went to paradise because that is where risen people belong. It is only through his resurrection that Christians can have a living hope, and that we can enter into that inheritance that can never perish, spoil or fade, which is kept in heaven for us. Of course, if Jesus did not rise, then it is all just false hope. The leader then encourages the group to ask if they want to explore any more about the resurrection of Jesus.

Finding purpose in life

A Christian woman is having a drink at the pub with her good friend who is not a believer. The friend is very successful in her job, very well paid and significantly senior in her organisation, and yet she is not in a peaceful place within herself. She says that she only really feels like she knows who she is when she is at work and busy, even though that is always a semi-stressful setting. She recognises the irony that she is so unhappy about the fact that she is only really anywhere near close to being happy when she is at work. In every other place, she is restless and unable to enjoy life. She would love to find joy in sitting at home reading a book or sitting at the kitchen counter fixing a broken appliance for the family, but she always carries a background anxiety if she is not actively sealing deals, hiring and firing, beating last year's figures and talking about all of these things with her colleagues while eating overpriced dinners at upmarket restaurants in her designer suits. Her Christian friend asks if she feels like a slave to her job and career. She does. She adds that she presumes that her Christian friend, who is nowhere near as successful or well-to-do, is far more relaxed and easy-going precisely because she is not trapped in a similar lifestyle. The Christian woman responds with a kind laugh, assures her friend that she too has plenty of stresses and challenges in her life and says that she is also trapped in a way, but intriguingly, she says that she is a very different kind of slave. She recounts that she recently noticed in her Bible that the Apostle Paul, one of the great founding leaders of the church, called himself a slave to Christ and that, as a Christian, she thinks that she is one too. She even pulls up Romans 1:1 on her phone and shows her friend the feature that says that the word rendered as 'servant' in this version of the Bible is better translated 'slave' from the original Greek text. The friend finds this mildly interesting (and actually finds it almost equally interesting that there are well-designed Bible apps and regular people who know something about different translations of the Bible). Mostly though, the friend is not very excited about being a slave to anything at the moment. The Christian woman agrees that it does not sound appealing at first, but she goes to explain that there is a deep paradox in the idea of being a slave to Christ. On the one hand, this means that she is bound to Jesus and his ways. But on the other hand, she finds there to be a profound underlying freedom in this because Jesus and his ways are deeply good for her. Recognising Jesus as the only Lord of all means that she does not ultimately have to strive to please anyone else, meet any social expectations or even measure up to her own best self. His yoke is easy and his burden is light (Matthew 11:28–30), far easier and lighter than any alternative that the world offers, as it turns out. She says that following someone who is as good and loving as Jesus is actually a joy that frees her from some of the pressures of life's many demands. With her eyes fixed on him, she has a deep peace, even as daily life remains somewhat chaotic and draining.

Feeding the flock on the gospel

A great thing that many churches, ministries and individual Christians do is continue to remind already faithful believers of the core of the gospel message. Once more, this can happen everywhere from large platform presentations to weekly Bible study groups right down to casual interpersonal conversations. Even our core gospel text, 1 Corinthians 15:3–5, opens up with a statement revealing that it is not being delivered evangelistically, but it is in fact a reminder of what the Corinthian Christians had already been well-instructed in. Paul obviously thought that there were occasions when it was absolutely essential to reiterate the basic gospel message to believers. This makes a lot of sense if the alternative is to forget, to practically forget or just to become distracted and sidetracked by other priorities – including other priorities of the life of faith, which can unfortunately become uncoupled from the gospel. It is possible, after all, for churches to get so wrapped up in everything from preparing liturgies, to strategic planning meetings, to filling rotas, to auditioning musicians, to running building projects, to organising kids' events that they can end up giving little time or attention to the gospel that is meant to be at the very heart of their existence.

But as much as it is correct to keep a focus on the gospel, this can also be mistakenly worked out. If drifting away from the gospel is one error to be avoided, so too is settling into a relatively predictable and unimaginative routine of gospel affirmation that never results in a growing knowledge of the breadth of God's revelation and never sees much progression in lived-out discipleship. Jesus does not want his followers to be unchanged over the course of their lives, believing that faithfulness does not expect much by way of maturation, sanctification and increases of knowledge and holy passions. Rather, he wants them to grow to become in every respect 'the mature body of him who is the head' (Ephesians 4:15).

Believers ought not simply seek to serve one another by forever finding the exact same gospel lesson in every single part of the Bible and then only encouraging stability at the expense of any proactive growth. Not only does this fail to do justice to the fullness of what God has revealed in the Scriptures, it also risks the perennial immaturity of God's people, as well as having them potentially growing bored and passive, feeling as though they have already received everything that God has for them and that they have already become everything that he wants them to be. As proper and necessary as it might be to underscore the fact that all Christians always and ongoingly rest solely on the grace of God for their righteousness before him, it is unlikely to be helpful or engaging to call a believer of a quarter of a century to urgent repentance every single week using the same texts, language and illustrations as those offered to seekers who know nothing substantial about Christianity. It is not good pastoral practice to continue to interact with people who have a longstanding faith in the same way as we would if they were people who had not yet made a decision for Christ. Ironically, the type of ministry commitment that always and only ever repeats the core of the gospel in a certain pre-formulated way might be the very thing that leads some Christians to seek elsewhere for something different that is more stimulating. And all of this is to say nothing about how the world around such Christians might end up under-served due to their lack of spiritual progress.

Fortunately, there is now no shortage of good Christian resources available to anyone who wants to continue growing in their spiritual maturity. A lack of books, courses and other materials is not the problem, although it might be the case that some wise guidance is needed to steer individuals to the resources that will most benefit them at their particular juncture in life. Having noted this, it is true that some of these materials on Christian living do not always aim for growth by drawing directly on the gospel or on a theology that is consciously anchored in the gospel. At worst, this can set up the mindset noted in chapter 7 that sees entry into the Christian life as coming through the gospel, but then growth as a follower of Jesus as coming through a focus on other things. In some cases, these materials can even be good things drawn from the wider life of faith, such as practical courses on the spiritual disciplines, encouragements from the lives of the heroes of the church's history or even insights on godliness and holiness taken from the Bible itself. Nonetheless, when these sorts of good things are not clearly framed as outworkings of the gospel, they can very easily become disassociated from it. The gospel can get passed over as the advancing Christian life is built up with other materials. Yet where that happens, there is an obvious question: how can anyone live a mature Christian life that is not always centred on the primary truths of the faith?

But if maturation does not come through repeated feeding with the most basic gospel 'milk', and ought not to come from engagement with anything that is not of the gospel (cf. 1 Corinthians 3:2; Hebrews 5:11–14), what is to be done? The good news is that it is unlikely that repetition of the gospel per se is what results in either immaturity or stagnation in the faith. Rather, those problems are more likely to be encountered when the same aspect of the gospel is repeated over and over, especially if it is always expressed the same way from many of the same biblical passages and is always seeking to tap into the same perceived felt needs. At best, this will just reinforce a part of the gospel and will not mature believers in the whole gospel. Thankfully, in this situation, there is an immediate opportunity for growth when the fullness of the gospel is recognised and seen to pervade the entirety of the Scriptures and to engage a wide range of felt needs. A believer who had formerly only ever heard the message of, say, new life through the resurrection of Christ will have a vast amount more to integrate into their understanding and living when they explore some of the depth of the message of the atonement and the divine messiahship of Jesus. Years of life-changing reflective, prayerful and exciting challenge lies before them without them moving an inch away from the heart of the gospel message.

Similarly, for those who do have a healthily rounded biblical gospel and desire to explore new and different dimensions of the faith, there is still no need to put the gospel to the side. Even when the diet becomes solid food rather than milk, it can always be solid gospel-food, or at least food that is thoroughly infused with the flavours of the gospel. Committing to things such as seeking justice in the world, developing better patterns of prayer, working towards more sacrificial financial support for Christian missions, training in mentoring, upskilling for more practical service in aspects of running church meetings, or anything else that might reflect Christian maturity can be the result of a deeper engagement with the gospel. And this maturation can come not only as a response to the good news (God has done that for me, so I had better do this for him) but also as a direct manifestation of the theologies of the gospel being lived out, as fuller expressions of atonement, eschatology, Christology or any of the other parts of Christian belief that ultimately tie back to the message of Jesus crucified and resurrected. Here, the gospel is not just the key to initial conversion, but to a complete renewal of mind and transformation of life with the ability to test and approve the good, pleasing and perfect will of God (Romans 12:2). A person who lives out their status as a saved, enslaved, hope-filled follower of holy King Jesus of Nazareth will enact justice as an agent of the living judge, will pray as a dependent of the one who rules over every aspect of creation and history, will give financially as a person who has no possessions of their own but only stewards what their master has entrusted to them, and so on. The gospel is not left behind, but it has become far more completely mind, heart, and life shaping.

In the brief examples below, three Old Testament texts are taken as starting points for illustrations of established Christians growing further, and each of these texts expresses a different part of the theology of the gospel. In the setting of the church community, these texts might be selected because the preacher recognises their utility for teaching on a particular point that the leadership thinks that the congregation needs to hear, but they could equally just come up as the text of the week in a long-range teaching programme that is systematically going through different books of the Bible. In the latter case, no pre-determined outcomes have been built into the choice of the text, but each passage is simply being listened to for what God has to say to his people from it. Once more though, we also know that much ministry happens away from the formal church service, and ongoing Christian maturation through further gospel engagement can happen in any number of settings.

God's unfailing love for those who should know better

A church is running a teaching series on the book of Ezekiel, preaching through it chapter by chapter each week in the Sunday services. The pastor comes naturally to chapter 16 as part of this. The text is quite confronting in its imagery: Jerusalem is personified, and her life is traced from being a discarded, blood-covered newborn baby, to being taken as the royal bride of God himself, to abandoning God and becoming an idol-worshipping, child-sacrificing, free prostitute of many nations, to being delivered over to the violent and abusive brutality of those same peoples, to the public shame of her own actions. But the chapter ends with God atoning for everything that Jerusalem has done and returning her, appropriately humbled, to her place as his special possession.

The preacher knows that most of the people in the congregation are believers, and so he does not need to teach them that God ultimately atones for the sins of the world through the death of Jesus – most of them will have made that connection for themselves when they heard the passage read before the sermon. Instead, he opens his sermon with a story about a non-Christian coming to faith when hearing about God's grace in Christ's death for the first time, but then he tacks to discuss those long-time believers who had regressed back into patterns of sin. He acknowledges that this is sometimes shocking because of the nature of the sin – something well-known in the congregation, where a case of adultery had recently come to light. But then, he pushes into those sins that often remain neatly secret and yet are utterly unfitting for God's people: pornography, gossip, selfishness, rudeness, laziness, rule bending. These are far too commonplace within the church, and they are not found on any of the Bible's lists of virtues.[2] The preacher asks if they are commonplace in the life of anyone in the congregation. He pushes deeper still and reflects upon how such attitudes and behaviours might be understandable in the life of someone who had not yet come to faith, but how supremely unfitting they would be for anyone who called him- or herself a follower of Jesus. He wants the church members to tap into any pushed-down awareness of ongoing sinfulness, even as declared followers of Jesus, and he wants them to feel this not just in concept ('Oh yes, none of us are without sins. That's just how it is this side of eternity.') but in reality, beating their breasts and ashamed even to look up to heaven, as in Luke 18:13. Of course, his goal is not to make his flock feel miserable and rejected – far from it! What he goes on to underscore at length is the fact that Christ's atoning death keeps them as God's special possession, even if they have settled into some sinful ways after receiving so much grace. The emphasis of this sermon is that God never stops loving his people and never breaks his covenant with them, even if their sins become worse than those of the most pagan of nations. There is no condemnation for those in Christ (Romans 8:1), including those in Christ who continue to struggle under real sin.

Confidence in God's great plans

A Bible study group is meeting together on an evening when a major public safety incident has unfolded nearby, and it is not at all certain whether things will settle back to normal soon or if they might get significantly worse and more widespread. There are some real concerns growing for everyone's security and the potential lasting consequences of what is going on. Rather than spending their whole time together speculating on what might happen next in this situation, the group leader decides that she will turn everyone to Joshua 4. Some members of the group feel quite distracted while reading it through, not seeing much immediate relevance of the story of Israel crossing the Jordan to enter the land of Canaan after their forty years of wandering in the wilderness. However, as they start discussing the passage together, it proves to be a blessing. They realise that the story is the critical complement to the record of the exodus out of Egypt. While the exodus and Red Sea crossing delivered God's people out of captivity and freed them to worship him, the Jordan crossing marks their entry into the promised land; it is their long-awaited arrival at their ultimate destination. They remember that God does not save his people to have them endlessly wander through their lives with all of their many challenges – which for the Israelites included military confrontations and worries about not having enough food – he also ultimately brings them to a place of security, abundance, stability and peace. They note that the promised land is a picture of heaven and the new creation, except that the new creation will be far better. After all, Israel could and did continue to get into all kinds of mess in their own land, and even they still needed a greater hope for their future.

All of God's people should be looking to the eternity that Christ has promised them, as there is no truly solid hope to be found anywhere else. The monument of twelve stones that Israel set up on the other side of the Jordan was to stand as a constant reminder that they had passed through the chaos of the waters to the other side on dry ground because of the Lord's protection. Likewise, in his resurrection, Christ sits at the right hand of his majestic Father and reminds his people that there is a better place after all of the strife of this life, and that he can bring them through (Hebrews 1:3). He has already passed over and been seen on the other side, where he is now preparing our lasting home for us (John 14:1–3).

Remembering your first love[3]

Two older believers are sitting together in a cafe enjoying a cup of coffee on a quiet Saturday morning. All is relatively well for both of them. They are in fair health, as are their families, home life is stable and neither one of them is currently dealing with major problems. One of them asks the other how his spiritual life is going, how his faith in Jesus is. The other replies that all is well enough there too. He is happy at church, where he is on a welcoming rota and occasionally does the Bible reading in the weekly service. He is part of a regular Bible study group, although some weeks he skips it because he appreciates a quiet night at home too. He sits comfortably with the church's statement of faith and feels it was appropriate for the elders to draw a couple of clear lines in a recent doctrinal dispute with some other local congregations.

But his friend decides to prod some more, to go beneath the surface. He asks him how he feels in his relationship with Jesus, whether there is a joy in knowing that he is loved by God, and whether he has a real passion for any of the church's current mission plans. The response is a long pause followed by a sober admission: not really. While he feels nothing at all negative towards the church, the truth is that he is not particularly engaged or excited by much to do with his faith. It is a fine part of his life that he would never want to let go of, but it is not something that puts a spring in his step or a twinkle in his eye. As much as he is personally convinced, he cannot imagine himself talking up the wonders of his relationship with Jesus in a conversation with a non-Christian.

His friend nods. He too has had seasons like this. But lately, he has been more fired up again. He flicks to his Bible app, finds Psalm 145 and reads it through right there. It is a psalm overflowing with praise of God. It refers to God's merciful works, but also to the splendour of his majesty and the fame of his abundant goodness. He says that when he first spent time thinking about it, the psalm seemed distant. It is, after all, in the voice of someone who is praising God as he was known before

Jesus' incarnation. But he says that that is what struck him in the end. After all, Jesus is God and King and is good and glorious in all of the ways that the psalm recounts. If what the psalm says is true of his King Jesus, then he is the loyal subject of this most awesome God, and there cannot be anything pedestrian about that. Initially, this was just a truth in his head that did not much impact his heart, but he took it on himself to read through one of the Gospels while at the same time remembering that the humble Jesus whom he found in its pages is also glorious and majestic in the ways that Psalm 145 describes. Over time, he recognised little shifts in his excitement and passion. At one point, he actually found himself smiling and tearing up as these thoughts were melding in his mind. How great to know such an awesome God. How great to belong to such an awesome King.

He asks his friend if he would be keen for them to read another of the Gospels together with the deliberate aim of stoking up their mutual joy at being people who have their identity in Jesus. The friend has just a pinch of healthy jealousy for the experience, and so he agrees.

*

Once more, all of the examples given in this chapter are imaginary, clipped and exploratory, and real life will never look exactly like any of them. And within any person or group of people, there will be different felt needs swimming around and jumbled up. Anyone seeking to share the Scriptures and the gospel with others at least needs to recognise this complexity and account for it as far as that is possible and practicable. Still, the examples hopefully show enough to demonstrate the potential usefulness of knowing the shape of the gospel and its theology for a fuller approach to both outreach and discipleship.

Of course, when ministering among a mixed group of non-Christians and believers, there will not only be a range of felt needs, but also the reality of very different standings before God and within the community of the church. Sometimes, when such mixed groups are addressed, an unhelpful 'us-and-them' perspective is communicated, with the 'us' being the believing church members and the 'them' being 'our non-Christian friends', 'people who have not yet responded to Jesus' or 'those we are hoping to invite to church'. If this sort of language is used, then any non-Christians who are present will feel that they are being openly spoken about rather than spoken to, and they are unlikely to find this very winsome. However, if the speaker directly shapes their words to address the non-Christians, an alternate issue could arise: those present who have been in the faith for a long time might feel ignored, as though the church or group is primarily interested in reaching outsiders rather than attending to the needs of committed members. Ironically, this can result in believers choosing not to show up at the times when they know that there is a deliberate plan to proclaim the gospel, as they feel that that will be an occasion that is not for them. Surely this cannot be a good thing. The solution to all of this is for the teacher to work hard at offering both milk and meat in the same serving of Scripture (cf. 1 Corinthians 3:2; Hebrews 5:11–14). They need to mine the texts for deeper gospel truths that will continually challenge those who might have heard the passages taught on many occasions, while at the same time making the lessons accessible for those coming to them with completely fresh ears.

Perhaps an analogy to this kind of teaching is the screening of a classic film that people love to rewatch many times because they always take joy in its beloved characters and famous big moments, and they also continually appreciate more and more of its depth and nuance. But at the same time, the film is riveting for the first-time viewer. Of course, it is not at all easy to produce a classic like this week after week, study after study. Nevertheless, sharing the Bible with a group, either formally or informally, should probably always be done with a mixed purpose and a mixed audience in mind. This is part of the challenge and rewarding richness of contributing to a more engaging gospel ministry.

A gracious gospel

The gospel is God's good news. And it is great news that the gospel is not an unknowable mystery and great news that the church at large has never lost the gospel. Additionally, despite its countless traumas, novelties, offshoots and re-creations over its twenty centuries, the Christian church, under God, has been successful in developing, solidifying and making mainstream a suite of doctrines that can be clearly traced back to the Bible. Thus, for all of the theological variation among different denominations and local congregations around the world today, it is still the case that there are churches in every place that hold to a set of beliefs and proclamations that the majority of Christians easily recognise and happily accept as true to the proclamation of the faith and the word of God. In short, under God, the global church has not in any concerning way lost, distorted or deprioritised the main messages of Jesus and the related teachings about him found in the Scriptures.

To be sure, there have always been erroneous beliefs that have gained traction in certain quarters of the church for certain periods, and there have been times when certain truths have been so much at the fore that others have slipped too far into the background. There have even been some wings of the church that have wandered off and settled down with quite different theological convictions than most. But it would be too much for anyone to say that the message of King Jesus crucified and risen has ever spent a long time away from the centre of the life of God's church as a whole.

Certainly, this book is not making any claim to have rediscovered the gospel. At most, it has only sought to reconfirm the biblical gospel that is already well established in the minds and communities of many Christians. Perhaps it has offered some useful suggestions on how to best seek out and crystallise that gospel and some thoughts on how to access and understand more of the Bible's theology that flows from, and culminates in, the amazing depths of the simple gospel truths.

Yet even as we celebrate the endurance and preservation of the gospel from the time of Jesus to today, and even as we have complete trust that God will oversee the protection and transmission of the gospel into the future, we must recognise our real responsibility to guard the good deposit of the faith proactively and share it with others uncorrupted (2 Timothy 1:14). Each new generation must be diligent in receiving and confirming the gospel and in closely studying the Bible to understand its gospel-shaped fullness before passing on what it can to those who will follow. After all, good theology is the most important legacy and truest heritage of the church. The most precious things that we can give to the next generations are not our properties, nor our financial holdings, nor the positions we might occupy in the structures of civil society, nor our cherished traditions, nor our operational processes. These are all truly important, but they are also only of secondary value to the church. The most precious things that we have and pass on are our beliefs. These are our oldest and most valuable possessions, which have been preserved, clarified and deepened since the time of Christ, and they need to be treasured by his people into eternity.

Looking at this from the negative perspective, we can say that it would be incredibly dangerous for the people of God to get his gospel completely wrong. If it were not, why would Paul warn against it so strongly in the opening of his Letter to the Galatians (Galatians 1:6–10)? Getting the gospel wrong, just like turning away from the gospel or deprioritising the gospel, offends and misrepresents God, who with grace has shared with us his priceless message of forgiveness and eternal life and even shared himself in the person of his Son. It also dishonours the Lord Jesus who gave us our lives at the cost of his own, something that we know is at the very heart of the substance of the gospel message. Jesus' descent from the heavens to the darkest depths for our sake surely warrants our constant holding of his message high, just as the Father has exalted him to the highest place (Philippians 2:9). And further still, getting the gospel wrong would also severely endanger the spiritual welfare of those who might end up hanging their hopes on a mistaken message that does not carry the promises of God. For them, it could be eternally ruinous. Getting the gospel wrong is dangerous, so getting the gospel right really matters.

Still, as much as we must maintain this priority of the New Testament, it must not be pushed to extremes. Maintaining a wise and gentle balance is critical. We could not, for instance, say that if a person – or even a whole church – could not crisply articulate the gospel in the fashion that this book has highlighted, then they are not properly Christian. That would be overly harsh and indeed not at all in line with the biblical witness. As we have repeatedly seen, the truths of the gospel are woven throughout the whole Bible, even if they are not always presented in a distilled, systematic form. The text and theology of the Scriptures are shot through with references and allusions to the lordship of Jesus, the need for and nature of atonement, and the hope and freedom of an eschatological future that is grounded in resurrection. The Bible is a gospel book, and the same can be true for people or churches too. Although it might prove difficult for some believers or believing communities to offer a well-grounded, neat and punchy gospel summary immediately, it can still be very much the case that they are thoroughly soaked in and incontestably shaped by the core truths of Jesus' rule, sacrifice and risen glory. Where this is evident in either individuals or groups, no fair case can be made for questioning their participation in the gospel purposes of God. To be sure, it will always be good for God's people to grow in theological sharpness and in their ability to articulate what they hold to be true. But recognising our common need for growth is different from suggesting that an inability to present the gospel in a certain way should raise concerns about whether someone or some church belongs to the faith.

The same needs to be said for many cases where we find one of the core gospel truths being elevated over the others. A church that puts special priority on, say, resurrection life should be embraced, even if there is room for a loving conversation about the equally proper place of Jesus' rule and death in their corporate convictions. This is also true for churches that might put atonement front and centre over messiahship and resurrection, or messiahship over atonement and resurrection. These would seem to be matters of emphasis rather than cases of outright gospel confusion. And as one church might be able to learn a better balance of gospel theology from the other, so the other needs to be open to any adjustments that it might need to make too. Even if there is an obvious plank in someone else's eye, we must still recognise the possibility of the tiniest speck in our own (cf. Matthew 7:3–5).

We should add at this point that Christians must never be shy about openly discussing the substance of our faith as we seek to build one another further up in the truth. Indeed, this should be part and parcel of everyday Christian living. If we are not helping one another to grow and refine our understanding of Jesus and his gospel through the words of the Bible, what are we doing in our preaching, Bible study groups, and one-to-one Bible reading and Christian relationships? Certainly, we must not retreat from such conversations for fear of being challenged in our faith or challenging others in theirs. We need to be more robust than that, secure in both the enduring love of God and the sisterly and brotherly love that we have for one another.

Going even further, it is also the case that we cannot be too quick to disown those who are way off track with the gospel through either having the message totally jumbled or through serious moral or doctrinal divergence. Consider the Corinthians, whose need to be reminded of the gospel is the reason that it is put so directly in front of us in the Scriptures. It seems that Paul had to be so painstakingly precise in laying out the gospel for this church because of how wrongly they had understood it at almost every level. Indeed, to their ongoing embarrassment, the Corinthian church stands as history's prime example of a church in all kinds of theological and moral mess! It needed to come back to the supremacy of Christ in all things (1 Corinthians 1–2). It needed to focus again on living sacrificially and following in the ways of the cross (1 Corinthians 3–14). It needed to re-understand the very nature of the resurrection (1 Corinthians 15). And these were not just intellectual or doctrinal problems for them; they were deeply ethical and spiritual too. The Corinthians were not living gospel-shaped lives at all. Yet for all of their serious departures from the gospel, Paul opens his letter by addressing them as those who are sanctified in Christ Jesus, and indeed collectively as the 'church of God' (1 Corinthians 1:2).

In a similar way, five of the seven churches profiled by Jesus in Revelation 2 and 3 had strayed from gospel purity, and yet he does not reject them. Instead, he calls them to correction in the expectation that they can be better aligned to his truth and ways. They are not 'synagogues of Satan', which is what he calls other gatherings of people who claim to belong to God, but who had completely rejected the message of his Messiah (Revelation 2:9, 3:9). The New Testament does not show us perfect Christians nor perfect churches that we are meant to measure up to. Rather, it shows us the fallible, flawed and faulty people of God, who need to keep hearing and relearning the gospel. They are models of all believers and all churches, and through them we see the ongoing patience and love of God towards his people, who are still sadly sinful and slow to completely embrace his good news on this side of eternity.

Even at the most basic levels of getting the gospel and gospel living right, all of us will fall short somewhere. Even those of us who do not stray away from the gospel well know that we are far from being thoroughly formed by it. As we have seen, the gospel is not only the simple truth that can be learned in moments and memorised easily enough; it also has such amazing depth that none of us will ever exhaust everything it has for us in either its theological richness or its purposes in shaping us as people of grace. Moreover, we have also seen that the gospel runs counter to many of our expectations and personal priorities such that even the smartest and purest of us will repeatedly struggle to conform our minds and lives to its truths. And, as God treats us, so we must also treat others.

In short, we must not join our firm embrace of gospel truths to a rigid requirement for everyone to articulate those truths sharply and in fine detail, and neither can we distance ourselves from other believers who see the balance of gospel truths differently. In such cases, we ought to be gracious in assuming that if they are not against us, then they are for us – or more importantly, if they are not against the gospel, then they are for God and God is for them (cf. Mark 9:38–40). Even so, at the same time, we must always seek to encourage one another to move forward in crisper, broader and deeper understandings of the gospel that translate into Christian lives and communities that more holistically embody the central truths of our faith. We ought to love one another so much that we do not quickly reject those who hold to beliefs that vary somewhat from our own, while at the same time seeking passionately to help one another grow in our grasp of God's good news, even as that might sometimes bring its challenges. The gospel is far too important for us not to do so.

*

In any short work, there is always a lot that cannot be covered, especially in a work that has not attempted to offer an even scholarly treatment of all of the subjects that it has touched upon. It could fairly be asked why certain themes or theological topics closely associated with the gospel have not been given more attention in this book. For example, we have said little about Paul's central concept of union with Christ, we have not gone deep into the category-flipping doctrines of grace, we have arguably been thin in using the language of the kingdom of God, and there has not been much on belief and faith, nor on the work of the Holy Spirit. With regard to the doctrines of belief and faith, aside from the fact that they each merit several standalone volumes, their thin treatment herein is because these might be better opened up in a consideration of the human response to the gospel rather than one focusing on the gospel message to which the response is made. While some evangelistic presentations of the gospel sensibly include the call to respond, as any complete gospel theology must do too, the present purpose has been to focus on the message rather than its impact, as wonderful as that is. For many of the other areas not covered, the very fact that they come to mind as we study the gospel underscores one of the key points of this book: all theology is interconnected with the gospel at the hub. It should be unavoidably clear that direct lines can be drawn from the grand themes of Scripture, such as the grace of God, to the simple gospel assertions of the death and resurrection of Jesus the Messiah. Indeed, if these connections are now being made more readily, and if we are now wanting more intently the links between every part of Christian theology and the gospel to be made, this book will have achieved one of its major aims.

Of course, while these sorts of connections – or at least the idea of them – is plain enough, a deeper question might be asked as to whether we have even made enough of the areas we have covered in the preceding pages. Perhaps for some, it is not enough to note that there is a meaningful connection between the kingdom of God and the gospel message because it is necessary to make the discussion of the kingdom of God central and expansive in any articulation of the Bible's main message. Ultimately though, this is a matter of theological interpretation and priority that cannot be absolutised. Of course, no one would want to suggest for half a moment that the kingdom of God is anything other than central to our fuller thinking about the gospel, and it is a blessing that so many excellent books have been written that go into far more depth than we have here.[4] And the same is true for all of the other big topics of Scripture: not everything can be said in one place, but we are privileged to have access to so many different resources to help us to keep increasing our understanding. Once more, the exciting thing is that the simple truth of the gospel has amazing depth, such that we can continue to dwell on it afresh, consider it in light of other doctrines, pray through it, shape our lives by it and praise God for it for the rest of our lives and into the eternity that our risen King Jesus has opened up for his saved people. All praise be to him.

Notes

Introduction

1 I am not making a case for authorship of the different biblical books. Whatever is concluded does not impact the present point.

2 See K. Stendahl, 'The Apostle Paul and the Introspective Conscience of the West', *Harvard Theological Review* 56 (1963), pp. 199–215; E. P. Sanders, *Paul and Palestinian Judaism* (Minneapolis: Fortress Press, 1977); J. D. G. Dunn, 'The New Perspective on Paul', *Bulletin of the John Rylands Library* 65.2 (1983), pp. 95–122.

3 cf. N. T. Wright's repeated challenge, 'We must stop giving 19th Century answers to 16th Century questions and begin giving 21st Century answers to 1st Century questions.' See, for example, David P. Seemuth, 'What I Learned from a Week with Professor Wright', https://www.ntwrightonline.org/what-i-learned-from-a-week-with-professor-wright/ (accessed 16 January 2025).

4 See, for example, D. A. Carson, P. T. O'Brien and M. A. Seifrid, *Justification and Variegated Nomism: The Complexities of Second Temple Judaism*, vol. 1 (Grand Rapids: Baker Academic, 2001); D. A. Carson, P. T. O'Brien and M. A. Seifrid, *Justification and Variegated Nomism: The Paradoxes of Paul*, vol. 2 (Grand Rapids: Baker Academic, 2004).

5 For example, the shift to narrative readings of theology in reaction against more cognitive-propositional theology as spearheaded by H. W. Frei, *The Eclipse of Biblical Narrative* (New Haven & London: Yale University Press, 1980) and G. A. Lindbeck, *The Nature of Doctrine* (Louisville: Westminster John Knox Press, 1984).

1 So. Many. Gospels

1 Throughout this volume, 'evangelical' refers to the trans-denominational theology, theologians and theological movement that are each committed to the inerrancy of Scripture and its primacy for determining doctrine and praxis. It does not infer any political convictions as it often can, particularly in the US.

2 See, for example, J. E. Rotelle (ed.) *The Works of Saint Augustine*, vol. 23, trans. R. J. Teske (New York: New City Press, 1997), pp. 225–75, cf. pp. 204–24.

3 See, for example, Acts 2:1–21; 1 Corinthians 1:26; Galatians 3:28, cf. Exodus 12:38, where many non-Israelites join the protonation from its very beginning.

4 On tribalism, see A. Chua, *Political Tribes* (New York: Penguin Random House, 2018); M. Volf, *Exclusion and Embrace*, rev. edn (Nashville: Abingdon Press, 2019).

5 In recognition of the bizarre and dangerous nature of this belief, in 2019, Princeton University's Office of Religious Life hosted a conference entitled, 'Christianity and White Supremacy', stating,'Christianity is one of the major supports of white supremacy and simultaneously its biggest challenge. The malformation of the Gospel of Jesus Christ into advocacy for white supremacy is heresy while the power of the Gospel is our greatest hope of vanquishing it.' See https://bit.ly/ChristianityandWhiteSupremacyConf (accessed 18 December 2024). White supremacy is an especially strange idea given that a significant question in the New Testament has to do with whether and how the non-Jewish peoples of the Mediterranean world could participate in a religion that started as a Jewish-dominated offshoot of Judaism.

6 A great many books on the phenomenon of Christian nationalism have appeared in the past few years, including P. D. Miller, *The Religion of American Greatness* (Downers Grove: IVP Academic, 2022); J. Wallis, *The False White Gospel* (New York: St Martin's Essentials, 2024); S. Bezner, *Your Jesus is too American* (Grand Rapids: Brazos Press, 2024). However, the idea of divinely privileged nations goes back to at least the Reformation. See, for example, W. Haller, *The Elect Nation* (New York: Harper & Row, 1963); K. R. Firth, *The Apocalyptic Tradition in Reformation Britain 1530–1645* (Oxford: Oxford University Press, 1979), pp. 107–9.

7 See, for example, D. B. Hart, *That All Shall be Saved* (New Haven & London: Yale University Press, 2019).

8 See Deuteronomy 6:14–15; Matthew 22:1–14; John 14:6; Acts 2:38; Romans 10:10–17; 2 Thessalonians 1:8–10.

9 Theologians call this 'the doctrine of divine simplicity'.

10 See Matthew 6:19–21; John 15:18–21; Hebrews 10:32–38.

11 Note particularly how the Beatitudes of Matthew 5:3–12 reshape the covenant blessings of Deuteronomy 28:2–8.

12 For a helpful introduction to the social gospel, see S. C. Shepherd, 'Social Gospel' in D. R. Goldfield (ed.), *Encyclopedia of American Urban History*, vol. 2 (Thousand Oaks: Sage Publications, 2007), pp. 738–40.

13 For an entire systematic theology framed around the social gospel, see W. A. Rauschenbusch, *Theology for the Social Gospel* (New York: The MacMillan Company, 1917).

14 The recent theological statement Social Justice and the Gospel, which is contentious in itself, seeks to set the theology of social justice in its right place so it does not compromise the gospel proper. See https://statementonsocialjustice.

com (accessed 18 December 2024), cf. S. D. Allen, *Why Social Justice is not Biblical Justice* (Grand Rapids: Credo House Publishers, 2020).

15 See, for example, M. F. Bird and J. Maston (eds), *Five Views on the Gospel* (Grand Rapids: Zondervan Academic, 2025).

16 See, for example, L. L. Morris, *The Apostolic Preaching of the Cross* (London: The Tyndale Press, 1955); L. L. Morris, *The Cross in the New Testament* (Grand Rapids: Eerdmans,1965); J. R. W. Stott, *The Cross of Christ*, 20th anniv. edn (Nottingham: Inter-Varsity Press, 2006).

17 J. R. W. Stott, *The Message of Acts* (Leicester: Inter-Varsity Press, 1990), p. 289, cf. J. R. W. Stott, *The Contemporary Christian* (Leicester: Inter-Varsity Press, 1992), p. 60.

18 J. R. W. Stott, *The Incomparable Christ* (Downers Grove: Inter-Varsity Press, 2001), pp. 60–1. This text gives a gospel presentation more akin to that which will be argued for in the next chapter.

19 M. J. Gorman, *Apostle of the Crucified Lord* (Grand Rapids & Cambridge: Eerdmans, 2004), p. 99. Emphasis original.

20 Interestingly, *sola crux* is not one of the five *solae* used to express Reformation theology.

21 C. H. Dodd, *The Apostolic Preaching and its Developments* (London: Hodder & Stoughton, 1963), p. 16.

22 Dodd, *Apostolic Preaching*, p. 21.

23 Dodd, *Apostolic Preaching*, p. 21.

24 Dodd, *Apostolic Preaching*, p. 21.

25 J. Dickson, *The Best Kept Secret of Christian Mission* (Grand Rapids: Zondervan, 2010), pp. 126–9. This is a popular version of Dickson's more technical *Mission Commitment in Ancient Judaism and the Pauline Communities* (Tübingen: Mohr Siebeck, 2003). That volume, however, does not include the exploration of the gospel.

26 Dickson, *Best Kept Secret*, p. 139.

27 While most can accept that Philippians 2:6–11 is an early hymn, there is no common mind regarding other texts such as Romans 4:25, 1 Corinthians 8:6 and 1 Peter 3:18. See, for example, D. Moo, *The Epistle to the Romans* (Grand Rapids: Eerdmans, 1996), p. 288; T. R. Schreiner, *Romans* (Grand Rapids: Baker Books, 1998), p. 243; G. D. Fee, *The First Epistle to the Corinthians*, rev. edn (Grand Rapids: Eerdmans, 2014), p. 413. cf. L. Goppelt, *A Commentary on 1 Peter*, trans. J. E. Alsup (Grand Rapids: Eerdmans, 1993), pp. 248–50; A. C. Thiselton, *The First Epistle to the Corinthians* (Grand Rapids: Eerdmans, 2000), pp. 635–8.

28 S. McKnight, *The King Jesus Gospel* (Grand Rapids: Zondervan, 2011), pp. 148–53.

29 McKnight, *King Jesus Gospel*, p. 153.

30 M. Dever, *The Gospel & Personal Evangelism* (Wheaton: Crossway, 2007), p. 43. cf. R. C. Sproul, *Getting the Gospel Right* (Grand Rapids: Baker Books, 1999), pp. 185–92.

31 Sometimes, this distinction is made as part of considerations of the doctrine of atonement. See, for example, F. W. Dillistone, *The Christian Understanding of Atonement* (London: SCM Press, 1984), p. 22: 'The distinction between "fact" and "interpretation" is of the greatest importance in any discussion of the doctrine of the Atonement for it corresponds to the distinction between "fact" and "theory" which has played so large a part in the history of the doctrine.'

32 cf. Stott, *The Cross of Christ*, p. 274: 'the resurrection was *the conquest confirmed and announced* … the cross was victory won, and the resurrection [was] victory endorsed, proclaimed and demonstrated.' Emphasis original.

33 McKnight, *King Jesus Gospel*, p. 152.

34 Dodd, *Apostolic Preaching*, p. 16.

35 J. R. Treat, *The Crucified King* (Grand Rapids: Zondervan, 2014).

36 N. T. Wright, *The Resurrection of the Son of God* (London: SPCK, 2003), p. 242.

37 Wright says different things in different places. For example, in N. T. Wright, *What Saint Paul Really Said* (Oxford: Lion Publishing, 1997), pp. 153–4, the gospel is only that Jesus is Lord, not *risen* Lord. In N. T. Wright, *Simply Good News* (London: SPCK, 2015), p. 82, the gospel is primarily about the death and resurrection of the Messiah.

2 The gospel from exegesis

1 For a fuller discussion of the trustworthy sayings, see G. W. Knight, *The Faithful Sayings in the Pastoral Letters* (Kampen: Kok, 1968); R. A. Campbell, 'Identifying the Faithful Sayings in the Pastoral Epistles', *Journal for the Study of the New Testament* 54 (1994), pp. 73–86.

2 cf. M. E. Gordley, *New Testament Christological Hymns* (Downers Grove: Inter-Varsity Press, 2018), chapter 1.

3 See, for example, J. R. Edwards, *The Gospel According to Mark* (Grand Rapids: Eerdmans, 2002), p. 23; R. T. France, *The Gospel of Mark* (Grand Rapids: Eerdmans, 2002), 51n4. cf. R. J. Kernaghan, *Mark* (Downers Grove: Inter-Varsity Press, 2007), pp. 28–9.

4 See, for example, R. H. Stein, *Mark* (Grand Rapids: Baker Academic, 2008), pp. 21–35. Stein sees the key themes of Mark as Christology, the 'Messianic Secret', the disciples, discipleship and the death of Jesus Christ. cf. M. A. Beavis, *Mark* (Grand Rapids: Baker Academic, 2011), pp. 22–4. Beavis finds Mark's overarching

concerns to be Jesus, the disciples, a nuanced presentation of Jews and Judaism, the response to Jesus and his message, suffering and loss, and the fulfilment of Old Testament Scripture.

5 See, for example, J. R. Donahue and D. J. Harrington, *The Gospel of Mark* (Collegeville: The Liturgical Press, 2002), pp. 59–60. Donahue and Harrington explain that the interpretation is somewhat a function of punctuation – whether a comma or a period ought to follow 'the Son of God'. For a concise overview of some of the different ways verse 1 functions, see C. B. E. Cranfield, *The Gospel According to St Mark* (Cambridge: Cambridge University Press, 1977), pp. 34–5.

6 For example, Edwards, *Gospel According to Mark*, p. 45; Stein, *Mark*, p. 72; Beavis, *Mark*, p. 43.

7 Compare, for example, the ESV, NASB, NLT and NRSV.

8 cf. L. T. Johnson, *The Acts of the Apostles* (Collegeville: The Liturgical Press, 1992), pp. 101, 103; W. J. Larkin, *Acts* (Leicester: Inter-Varsity Press, 1998), p. 98; D. L. Bock, *Acts* (Grand Rapids: Baker Academic, 2007), p. 253. For the relation of teaching and proclaiming in this verse, see C. S. Keener, *Acts: An Exegetical Commentary*, vol. 2 (Grand Rapids: Baker Academic, 2013), pp. 1245–6.

9 For example, C. E. B. Cranfield, *Romans* (Grand Rapids: Eerdmans, 1985), p. 1; Moo, *Epistle to the Romans*, p. 40; Schreiner, *Romans*, pp. 37–45; N. T. Wright, 'The Letter to the Romans: Introduction, Commentary, and Reflections' in *The New Interpreter's Bible*, vol. X (Nashville: Abingdon, 2002), pp. 415–19; G. R. Osborne, *Romans* (Downers Grove: Inter-Varsity Press, 2004), pp. 29–32; F. J. Matera, *Romans* (Grand Rapids: Baker Academic, 2010), pp. 29–30; C. G. Kruse, *Paul's Letter to the Romans* (Grand Rapids: Eerdmans, 2012), pp. 41–7. D. Robinson, *Faith's Framework*, 2nd edn (Blackwood: New Creation Publications, 1996), p. 60 asserts without argument that 'Paul's most comprehensive definition of the gospel is in the opening of Romans.'

10 Although see Wright, 'Letter to the Romans', pp. 416–17; V. S. Poythress, 'Is Romans 1:3–4 a Pauline Confession after All?', *The Expository Times* 87 (1975–1976), p. 180. cf. S. E. Porter, *The Letter to the Romans* (Sheffield: Phoenix Press, 2015), p. 45.

11 See, for example, W. Hendriksen, *I & II Timothy & Titus* (Edinburgh: Banner of Truth Trust, 1957), p. 251.

12 cf. P. H. Towner, *The Letters to Timothy and Titus* (Grand Rapids: Eerdmans, 2006), pp. 499–501.

13 cf. P. W. Barnett, *1 Corinthians* (Fearn: Christian Focus Publications, 2000), p. 272; A. C. Thiselton, *First Epistle to the Corinthians*, p. 1189; D. E. Garland, *1 Corinthians* (Grand Rapids: Baker Academic, 2003), p. 684; R. E. Ciampa and B. S.

Rosner, *The First Letter to the Corinthians* (Grand Rapids: Eerdmans, 2010), p. 746; G. D. Fee, *First Epistle to the Corinthians*, p. 803. J. Dickson, *The Best Kept Secret of Christian Mission* (Grand Rapids: Zondervan, 2010), p. 117 sees five points, adding in Jesus' identity as the Christ as essential to the message.

14 This layout works equally as neatly in the original Greek as it does in the English translation.

15 Dickson, *Best Kept Secret*, pp. 120–1 is perhaps unconvincing in trying to demonstrate that the burial of Jesus is of comparable theological significance to his death.

16 Martin Hengel speaks directly to the relationship between the gospel as narrated in the written Gospels and the gospel as a doctrinal message of salvation and Christology in M. Hengel, *The Four Gospels and the One Gospel of Jesus Christ* (London: SCM Press, 2000), esp. chapter 5. He sees the relationship not only as propositions drawn from narratives, but narratives supplied to explain the propositions. See also S. Gathercole, *The Gospel and the Gospels* (Grand Rapids: Eerdmans, 2022).

17 cf. Matthew 17:22–23, 20:18–19; Mark 8:31, 9:31, 10:33–34; Luke 9:22, 43b–45, 18:31–33.

3 What actually happened: the two gospel events

1 M. Hengel, *Crucifixion*, trans. J. Bowden (London: SCM Press, 1977); see also F. Rutledge, *The Crucifixion* (Grand Rapids: Eerdmans, 2017), chapter 2.

2 The NIV has slightly obscured these connections, not only rendering the 'tree' (עץ) of Deuteronomy 21:22 as 'pole' but also rendering 'tree' (ξύλου) as 'cross' in Acts 13:29. In Galatians 3:13, it gives 'pole' for ξύλου, presumably to match the verse in Deuteronomy.

3 J. Moltmann, *The Crucified God*, trans. R. A. Wilson and J. Bowden (London: SCM Press, 1974), p. 243. Note that Moltmann is not promoting patripassianism – the idea that the Father suffers on the cross – but rather that the Father has his own distinct suffering because of the Son's.

4 See, for example, P. T. Nimmo and K. L. Johnson (eds), *Kenosis* (Grand Rapids: Eerdmans, 2022). cf. B. L. McCormack, *The Humility of the Eternal Son* (Cambridge: Cambridge University Press, 2021).

5 Calvin, J. *The Institutes of the Christian Religion*, 2.13.4.

6 Calvin, *Institutes*, 2.14.1ff.

7 Calvin, *Institutes*, 2.14.2.

8 https://thewestminsterstandard.org/the-chalcedonian-creed/ (accessed 10 January 2025).

9 N. T. Burns, *Christian Mortalism from Tyndale to Milton* (Cambridge MA: Harvard University Press, 1972).

10 For example, Mark 12:30; Luke 1:46–47; Romans 8:1–17; 1 Thessalonians 5:23.

11 'The Chalcedonian Definition', https://thewestminsterstandard.org/the-chalcedonian-creed/ (accessed 10 January 2025). cf. Article 19 of the Belgic Confession, which in part says, 'But these two natures are so closely united in one person, that they were not separated even by his death. Therefore that which he, when dying, commended into the hands of his Father, was a real human spirit, departing from his body. But in the meantime the divine nature always remained united with the human, even when he lay in the grave. And the Godhead did not cease to be in him, any more than it did when he was an infant, though it did not so clearly manifest itself for a while.' https://thewestminsterstandard.org/the-belgic-confession/ (accessed 10 January 2025).

12 cf. for example, R. Bultmann, *Kerygma and Myth* (SPCK, 1953), pp. 38–43; P. Carnley, *The Structure of Resurrection Belief* (Oxford: Clarendon Press, 1987), pp. 16ff, 352–68.

13 For example, J. McDowell, *The New Evidence that Demands a Verdict* (Nashville: Thomas Nelson Publishers, 1999), pp. 203–84; G. Habermas, 'The Resurrection of Jesus and Recent Agnosticism' in N. L. Geisler and C. V. Meister (eds) *Reasons for Faith* (Wheaton: Crossway Books, 2007), pp. 281–94; W. L. Craig, *On Guard* (Colorado Spirings: David C. Cook, 2010), pp. 219–64.

14 For example, Wright, *Resurrection of the Son of God*, pp. 706–10.

15 See Matthew 26:67, 27:26, 30; Mark 14:65, 15:15, 19; Luke 22:63, 23:16, 22; John 18:22, 19:1–3. cf. also Jesus' passion predictions in the Gospels, for example, Matthew 16:21, 20:19.

16 See the Catechism of the Catholic Church online at https://www.vatican.va/archive/ENG0015/__P1R.HTM (accessed 19 December 2024).

17 See W. Grudem, 'He Did Not Descent into Hell: A Plea for Following Scripture Instead of the Apostles' Creed', *Journal of the Evangelical Theological Society* 34.1 (1991), pp. 103–14.

18 For example, T. Patrick, *Establishment Eschatology in England's Reformation* (London & New York: Routledge, 2024), pp. 26–8.

19 cf. M. J. Erickson, *Christian Theology*, 3rd edn (Grand Rapids: Baker Academic, 2013), p. 710. Erickson suggests that Christ was only transformed upon his ascension to heaven.

20 Interestingly, the only New Testament use of the same word for 'form' (μορφῇ) comes in Philippians 2:6–7, discussing the incarnation, the other moment of great physical change for the Second Person of the Trinity. For some of the discussions

around the term μορφῇ, see D. Macleod, *The Person of Christ* (Downers Grove: Inter-Varsity Press, 1998), pp. 212–13.

21 The NIV leaves out the 'then' (οὖν), which shows the disciples' rejoicing follows Jesus' showing his wounds.

22 Matthew 28:9 is the exception to the overall pattern, as it reports the women worshipping at the risen Jesus' feet the moment that they first encounter him and he greets them.

23 Wright coins the term 'transphysical' for the resurrection body in *Resurrection of the Son of God*, p. 477, cf. G. Vos, *The Pauline Eschatology* (Phillipsburg: Presbyterian and Reformed Publishing, 1930), pp. 155–6.

24 This is an idea imaginatively explored in C. S. Lewis, *The Great Divorce*, rev. edn (New York: HarperOne, 2015).

4 The theological meaning of the gospel

1 A. J. Johnson, *Atonement: A Guide for the Perplexed* (London & New York: T&T Clark, 2015), p. 105.

2 G. Aulén, *Christus Victor*, trans. A. G. Hebert (London: SPCK, 1965).

3 Aulén, *Christus Victor*, p. 4.

4 N. T. Wright, *Evil and the Justice of God* (London: SPCK, 2006), pp. 88–9.

5 F. Rutledge, *The Crucifixion* (Grand Rapids: Eerdmans, 2015), p. 392. Emphasis original. Quoting G. O. Forde, *A More Radical Gospel* (Michigan & Cambridge: Eerdmans, 2004), p. 88.

6 G. A. Cole, 'Eschatology' in A. J. Johnson (ed.), *T&T Clark Companion to Atonement* (London & New York: T&T Clark, 2021), p. 474.

7 A. E. McGrath, *The Christian Theology Reader*, 5th edn (Chichester: John Wiley & Sons), p. 299, quoting P. Abelard, *Expositio in Epistolam ad Romanos*. See also McGrath's commentary.

8 McGrath, *Christian Theology Reader*, p. 299.

9 See F. Schleiermacher and P. T. Nimmo, *The Christian Faith*, 3rd edn (London & New York: Bloomsbury T& T Clark, 2016).

10 Anselm of Canterbury, *Cur Deus Homo?*, 1.11. cf. Rutledge, *Crucifixion*, pp. 146–66; K. Sonderegger, 'Anselmian Atonement' in Johnson, *Companion to Atonement*, pp. 175–93.

11 Aquinas, T. *Summa Theologiae*, 3.48.2.

12 For example, Calvin, J. *Institutes of the Christian Religion*, 2.16.6. Some would carve out penal substitutionary atonement as a separate type of atonement theory altogether. For one full modern treatment of the doctrine in light of its detractors, see S. Jeffery, M. Ovey and A. Sach, *Pierced for our Transgressions: Rediscovering*

the Glory of Penal Substitution (Wheaton: Crossway, 2007). For a critical dialogue on the achievements of the cross, including engagement around the question of substitutionary atonement, see N. T. Wright, S. Gathercole and R. B. Stewart, *What Did the Cross Accomplish?* (Louisville: Westminster John Knox Press, 2021).

13 P. Melanchthon, 'Loci Communes Theologici' in W. Pauck (ed.), *Melanchthon and Bucer* (Philidelphia: The Westminster Press, 1969), p. 87.

14 Part two of Jeffrey, Ovey and Sachs, *Pierced for our Transgressions*, presents and then directly addresses many of the common objections to penal substitutionary atonement.

15 J. Moltmann, *In the End – the Beginning*, trans. M. Kohl (London: SCM Press, 2004), pp. 69–70.

16 cf. M. F. Bird, *Evangelical Theology*, 2nd edn (Grand Rapids: Zondervan Academic, 2020), pp. 466–75. Bird argues for *Christus Victor* as the most central theory of atonement.

17 E. W. Bullinger, *Word Studies on the Holy Spirit* (Grand Rapids: Kregel Publications, 1979), p. 115. Emphasis original.

18 R. B. Gaffin, *Resurrection and Redemption*, 2nd edn (Phillipsburg: Presbyterian and Reformed Publishing, 1987), p. 116.

19 Irenaeus, *Against Heresies*, 2.28.1, 3.22.3, 5.1.3.

20 For example, D. Farrow, *Ascension Theology* (London & New York: T&T Clark, 2011), pp. 36, 122.

21 cf. W. Pannenberg, *Jesus, God and Man*, 2nd edn, trans. L. L. Wilkins and D. A. Priebe (Philadelphia: The Westminster Press, 1977), pp. 390–7.

22 cf. N. T. Wright, *Surprised by Hope* (London: SPCK, 2007), pp. 78–9.

23 See O. O'Donnovan, *Resurrection and Moral Order*, 2nd edn (Grand Rapids: Eerdmans, 1994).

5 Why the gospel needs the God-man

1 Examples of early heresies that underplayed Jesus' divinity are Ebionitism and Arianism. Those that underplayed his humanity included Docetism and Appollinarianism.

2 See Genesis 6:2, 4; Psalm 82:6. cf John 8:1–39; Hosea 1:10.

3 See Matthew 16:21, 17:22–23, 20:18–19; Mark 8:31, 9:31, 10:33–34; Luke 9:22, 43b–45, 18:31–33.

4 'The Chalcedonian Definition', https://thewestminsterstandard.org/the-chalcedonian-creed/ (accessed 10 January 2025).

5 Calvin, *Institutes*, 2.16.12.

6 See the footnote on this text in any modern Bible.

7 See chapter 5.

8 'Question 23: Why must the Redeemer be truly God?', https://newcitycatechism.com/new-city-catechism/#23 (accessed 16 January 2025). This catechism is based on the various Protestant catechisms of the Reformation.

9 G. A. Cole, 'Eschatology' in A. J. Johnson (ed.), *T&T Clark Companion to Atonement*, p. 474.

10 There is a question as to whether it can be confirmed that Jesus ministered or died in a Jubilee Year as strictly calculated from the days of Moses. Nonetheless, it seems clear from Luke 4:19 – where Jesus quotes Isaiah 61:2, which in turn refers back to Leviticus 25:10–13 – that he is at least proclaiming a symbolic or spiritual Jubilee.

11 cf. A. C. Thiselton, *First Epistle to the Corinthians*, p. 40; G. D. Fee, *First Epistle to the Corinthians*, pp. 17–18.

12 This would be a brave conclusion to reach even from 2 Peter 1:4.

13 Anselm of Canterbury, *Cur Deus Homo?* 1.5. also notes that humanity is rightly indebted to the one who rescues it from eternal death.

6 The clearly predicted and completely unexpected gospel

1 There are countless texts on biblical hermeneutics that address these concepts. Some accessible and helpful volumes include G. K. Beale, *Handbook on the New Testament Use of the Old Testament* (Grand Rapids: Baker Academic, 2012); C. J. H. Wright, *Knowing Jesus Through the Old Testament*, 2nd edn (Carlisle: Langham Preaching Resources, 2014); J. M. Hamilton, *Typology* (Grand Rapids: Zondervan Academic, 2022). See also A. Malone, *Knowing Jesus in the Old Testament?* (Nottingham: Inter-Varsity Press, 2015).

2 For example, Exodus 12:37–38; Joshua 2, 6:16–17; Ruth 1–4; Acts 21:27–29.

3 For example, Matthew 12:1–13; Mark 7:1–23; Acts 10:9–16, 15:1–35.

4 See, for example, M. J. Vlach, *Dispensationalism* (Los Angeles: Theological Studies Press, 2017).

5 These issues are addressed in some of the conversations on the New Perspective on Paul, noted in the introduction.

6 For example, Matthew 8:17; Luke 22:37; John 12:38; Acts 8:32–33; Romans 10:16, 15:21; 1 Peter 2:22–25.

7 For example, J. R. Edwards, *Gospel According to Mark*, p. 327; R. T. France, *Gospel of Mark* p. 420; R. H. Stein, *Mark*, p. 488.

8 See also 2 Maccabees 7.

9 See chapter 5.

10 cf. J. E. Goldingay, *Daniel* (Dallas: Word, Incorporated, 1989), pp. 308–9; E. C. Lucas, *Daniel* (Leicester: Apollos, 2002), pp. 295–6.

11 See chapter 5.

12 See B. S. Rosner, *How to Find Yourself* (Wheaton: Crossway, 2022).

13 This is a development of Irenaeus' notion of the Son and Spirit as the 'two hands' of God. See *Against Heresies* 4, preface; C. E. Gunton, *The Promise of Trinitarian Theology*, 2nd edn (Edinburgh: T&T Clark, 1997), pp. xxvi–xxviii; C. E. Gunton, *Father, Son and Holy Spirit* (London & New York: T&T Clark, 2003), pp. 30–1. cf. for example, Matthew 5:1–2; John 3:8.

7 The gospel and gospel theology

1 Tim Keller's body of work is strong on this point.

2 See E. Ferguson, *The Rule of Faith* (Eugene: Cascade Books, 2015).

3 For example, H. L. Poe, *The Gospel and its Meaning* (Grand Rapids: Zondervan, 1996), pp. 44–52; D. Robinson, *Faith's Framework*, 2nd edn (Blackwood: New Creation Publications, 1996), pp. 12–14, 48–49.

4 C. A. Evans, 'The Function of the Old Testament in the New' in S. McKnight (ed.), *Introducing New Testament Interpretation* (Grand Rapids: Baker, 1990), p. 193. We are pushing this further to say that it is the hermeneutical key for our interpretation and application of both the Old and New Testaments.

5 M. F. Bird, *Evangelical Theology*.

6 Bird, *Evangelical Theology*, p. 37.

7 Even while affirming the centrality of penal substitutionary atonement, Bird gives the resurrection of Christ equal importance. See *Evangelical Theology*, pp. 456–66, 494–5.

8 D. A. Carson, 'Current Issues in Biblical Theology: A New Testament Perspective', *Bulletin for Biblical Research* 5 (1995), p. 17. cf. C. H. H. Scobie, *The Ways of our God* (Grand Rapids: Eerdmans, 2003), p. 5.

9 For a concise yet thorough history biblical theology, see, for example, A. J. Köstenberger and G. Goswell, *Biblical Theology* (Wheaton: Crossway, 2023), 1–8.

10 For example, Köstenberger and Goswell, *Biblical Theology*, pp. 1–2, 7, cf. 24–7.

11 P. Melanchthon, 'Dedicatory Letter' in 'Loci Communes Theologici' in W. Pauck, *Melanchthon and Bucer*, p. 21.

12 cf. T. Patrick and A. Reid, *The Whole Counsel of God* (Wheaton: Crossway, 2020), 98–101.

8 The whole gospel meets the whole problem of sin

1 The difficult questions include *why do we need a new Adam, but not a new Eve? is original guilt fundamentally unjust?* and *whence Adam and Eve's concupiscence?* Helpful texts on the doctrine of original sin, its history and different expositions include P. F. Beatrice, *The Transmission of Sin* (Oxford: Oxford University Press, 2013); H. Madueme and M. Reeves (eds), *Adam, the Fall, and Original Sin* (Grand

Rapids: Baker Academic, 2014); H. Blocher, *Original Sin* (Downers Grove: IVP Academic, 2020); J. B. Stump and C. Meister (eds), *Original Sin and the Fall* (Downers Grove: IVP Academic, 2020).

2 T. Patrick, *Establishment Eschatology in England's Reformation* (London & New York: Routledge, 2024), pp. 59–60.

3 See Psalm 62:12; Proverbs 24:12 Ecclesiastes 12:14; Romans 2:6; 2 Corinthians 5:10; Revelation 21:1–8.

4 For many people, the language of slavery immediately brings to mind the enslavement of Black Africans by white Britons and Americans. While we give thanks to God for the abolition of this practice, Black market slavery is still shockingly common today. For further information, see, for example, www.ijmuk.org (accessed 8 January 2025).

5 For slavery to Christ, see, M. J. Harris, *Slave of Christ* (Leicester: Apollos, 1999), esp. pp.139–56; M. J. Brown, 'Paul's use of δούλος Χρίστου Ἰησου in Romans 1:1', *Journal of Biblical Literature* 120.4 (2001), pp. 723–37; J. K. Goodrich, 'From Slaves of Sin to Slaves of God: Reconsidering the Origin of Paul's Slavery Metaphor in Romans 6', *Bulletin for Biblical Research* 23.4 (2013), pp. 509–30.

6 It is noteworthy that more than half of the steps in Alcoholics Anonymous's famous twelve-step programme reference a higher power. Clearly, this power is seen as necessary to end the addiction.

7 For example, Romans 1:1; Philippians 1:1; Titus 1:1. cf. James 1:1.

8 See, for example, S. McKnight and J. B. Modica (eds), *Jesus is Lord, Caesar is Not* (Downers Grove: IVP Academic, 2013).

9 M. W. Bates, *Salvation by Allegiance Alone* (Grand Rapids: Baker Academic, 2017) argues that the Greek word underlying the English 'faith' (πίστις) can also be rendered 'allegiance', meaning that justification requires allegiance to Jesus. While there is some merit to the translation and the theological concept, Bates probably overplays the idea to the detriment of the other legitimate senses of πίστις.

10 A. E. McGrath, *Christian Theology: An Introduction*, 6th edn (Chichester: John Wiley & Sons, 2017), pp. 331–2 notes that in Augustine's understanding, one of the three key concepts explaining sin is as a power that holds us captive. The other two are that it is a hereditary disease, and a judicial crime. These three overlap neatly with the categories discussed in the main text.

11 See chapter 5.

9 The gospel and practical ministry

1 H. Mackay, *Why Don't People Listen* (Sydney: Macmillan Australia, 2013), chapter 1.

2 cf. J. Bridges, *Respectable Sins* (Colorado Springs: NavPress, 2007).

3 cf. Revelation 2:4.

4 See, for example, G. E. Ladd, *The Gospel of the Kingdom* (Grand Rapids: Eerdmans,1959); P. Schreiner, *The Kingdom of God and the Glory of the Cross* (Wheaton: Crossway, 2018); N. Perrin, *The Kingdom of God* (Grand Rapids: Zondervan, 2019).

GREAT BOOKS
ARE EVEN BETTER WHEN THEY'RE SHARED

Help other readers find this one:
Post a review at your favourite online bookseller.

Post a picture on social media to share withothers. Tag us and we'll share your post on our own platforms.

Send a note to a friend who would also love it or, better yet, gift them a copy!

THANK YOU FOR READING

Discover more great books at
spckpublishing.co.uk